RAINDOG
LUMMOX Press

BROKEN LINES

THE ART & CRAFT OF POETRY

JUDITH SKILLMAN

PO Box 5301
San Pedro, CA 90733
www.lummoxpress.com

Printed in the United States of America

for Beth Bentley—

Poet, Teacher, Mentor

Acknowledgements

I am grateful to the following periodicals and anthologies, where these interviews and essays first appeared:

Interview with Jeremy Voigt, *Centrum Experience Magazine*, September, 2008. Editors Jordan Hartt and Jeremy Voigt.

"The Fine Art of Revision" and "Revising Your Manuscript for Theme*." Women on Poetry,* edited by Carol Smallwood, Colleen S. Harris, and Cynthia Brackett-Vincent. *McFarland Press*, North Carolina, 2012.

My gratitude to the Richard Hugo House in Seattle, Washington, for the opportunity to teach classes that resulted in the creation of some of the materials for this book.

Thanks to my students, clients, and colleagues in manuscript revision services and workshops, who taught me so much. I can name only a few here: Irene Bloom, Roberta Feins, Carol Ruth Kelly, Meredith Kunsa, Lawrence Matsuda, Keith Odett, Barbara Molloy, Stanley Niamatali, Matthew Silverman, and Mark Simpson.

To my colleagues in poetry who have given me support and unflagging encouragement, I owe a debt that can't be measured in any conventional fashion: Christianne Balk, Janée J. Baugher, Erika Carter, Eileen Duncan, Arthur Ginsberg, Pamela Gross, Sharon Hashimoto, Pat Hurshell, Susan Lane, Kurt Olsson, Anne Pitkin, Michael Spence, Joannie Stangeland, Barbara L. Thomas, and Lillo Way.

Thanks to Joannie Stangeland for her expert assistance with the section titled "Guidelines for Breaking Lines in Verse," as well as her guidance regarding revisions of the manuscript.

Thanks to Tom Skillman, who provided invaluable technical support and expertise.

For their specific suggestions, editing, and sage advice, special thanks to:

RD Armstrong
Christianne Balk
Janée J. Baugher
Erika Carter
Dr. Bernice Kastner
Carter Monroe
Raundi K. Moore-Kondo
Robbi Nester
Anne Pitkin
Tom Skillman
Joannie Stangeland

"Everything in life is writable about
if you have the outgoing guts to do it,
and the imagination to improvise.
The worst enemy to creativity
is self-doubt."

—Sylvia Plath

Contents

Contents *(continued)*

3. THE SPARK: COLLABORATION AND INSPIRATION

4. YOUR POETRY MANUSCRIPT

5. MAINTAINING MOTIVATION

SUPPORTING MATERIALS

Preface

What makes poetry its own medium apart from prose is, ultimately, the line break. It is therefore not surprising that theories regarding where the line breaks should occur come in all forms, and, in fact, every rule is broken once one moves from theory to practice.

For a sampling of these theoretical rulings, we can turn to Richard Hugo, who came down hard against breaking lines on little words: those pronouns, articles, and transitional words that belong with the verbs and/ or nouns they modify (*The Triggering Town*, 37.) And it was the Northwest's beloved Stafford who noted that a non-smoking sign in his office received a different kind of attention once it had broken lines, i.e., the appearance, if not the full impact, of a poem: "Please/ consider others/Smoking may shorten their lives/and may deprive them/ of your living presence" (*Writing the Australian Crawl*, 61.)

Perhaps not surprisingly, the many different takes on where to break a line can be used, metaphorically speaking, to take the discussion of where a line is broken in any given poem into an entirely new realm—where the poet, whose job it is to break lines—begins to feel, through his or her own line breaks, a certain connection to his or her influences. Given there is an "anxiety of influence" as Harold Bloom so eloquently elaborated; nonetheless, there must also exist a flip side to this dilemma, and that is the side that deserves our attention. It is the application of one's personal theories on the craft of making a poem that grow and evolve as the poet develops his or her voice.

Whether the product of that work is lyric or narrative, free or formal verse, becomes, finally, not as important as the recognition factor. The voice of poetry is strangely unique. If I am teaching several poets, it takes only one or two readings of one or two poems by an individual before I will come to recognize the next piece as that person's work without their name stamped on it. And this gift of recognition comes apart from handwriting, in today's age of word processing.

There remains a persistent question: how are poets to survive without recognition and income? For the large majority, there is none, and yet the field grows more crowded every year. Perhaps it is the implicit reward of making the work, though poets themselves don't often stop to praise this aspect of their lonely avocation. Certainly there appear to be more poets practicing in the 21st century than ever before. While the burgeoning presence of the world wide web has played an undeniable role in fostering this phenomena, as has the 'information age,' in which any subject can yield to soft research merely by clicking on Wikipedia, or Googling the appropriate term, there are other forces at play in the rising number of practicing poets.

Where once exercising one's creativity in a self-indulgent manner was frowned upon, it is now not only welcomed but encouraged at many universities throughout the country, with degrees such as the M.A., the MFA, the low residency MA and/or MFA, and even, despite the decline of liberal arts colleges in general, "poets in the schools," formerly heretical practitioners who enter the classroom to foster an appreciation of the art in public and private schools, sometimes even at the elementary school level. Poetry workshops are held in prisons and facilities for juvenile delinquents.

Perhaps all of this can be seen as an embarrassment of riches. Can there can be too much of a good thing? How is the beginning, or even the advanced student of poetry and poetics, to carve out his or her identity, given the sheer number of fellows who also produce work and with whom this young, middle-aged, or other demographic poet/poetess must compete? How justify one's existence when so many peers, predecessor, mentors, and colleagues can be found at any of the thousand conferences going on around the US and abroad?

We can give ourselves permission to be "the little god who makes order out of chaos," because, in doing so, we are simply echoing creation, whatever faith or belief system one subscribes to. Honoring the broken line requires, in some form, taking some or all of three "golden rules" as time allows, each and every time we take pen to paper or fingers to keyboard:

1. Giving ourselves permission to copy and define our own work by the immediate attention to authors whose compositions we admire. As visual artists are encouraged to find out how a certain painter achieved his or her effects by directly copying the work of art, so writers must do as well. This requires paying homage to our ancestry—it requires operating not under Bloom's "The Anxiety of Influence"— rather, embracing "The Ecstasy of Influence."

2. Observing our debt to fellow contemporary poets regardless of their "status" vs. our own— even better, doing away with any concept of a hierarchy and/or pecking order, and any competitive spirit other than the friendly, sportsman-like variety.

3. Linking form and content as we perceive it, not as we believe it should be "sold." For just

as art and craft are both necessary to every work in progress, style and form must marry content and subject matter. Awareness of these aspects can make a difference, enabling the poet to find his or her original voice rather than becoming just another spin-off on the current trend or fad in poetry.

Ultimately, it becomes the work of the poet to mend the broken line in all his or her overtures and ventures with language. Language is alive, which means it's always changing. Therefore, language embodies otherness. Its relationship to our lives predicts and acts as an indicator of our ability to become part of the world or to live in exile, not that one is preferable to the other. For the poet—*makeris*—"maker," in the Greek, labors wherever and however s/he can. It is the blessing and curse of self-knowledge to own the fact that one must create on one's own terms.

Ways in which I will touch on the broken line include the collation of some guidelines for line breaks, how to vary structure in the context of free verse, a scholarly seeking for the *ars poetica* poem, and the steps required to facilitate the act of coming out of the closet, which is a necessary part of reclaiming the creative self. A few excerpts of interviews have been included. They will, I trust, be taken lightly. Finally, I salute the art of collaboration with artists working in other mediums, and describe methods for maintaining motivation and fighting against the isolation (and subsequent depression) that is an occupational hazard of writing poems.

This book is not a textbook in the traditional sense. It is, quite simply, my personal take on ways and means that may assist both aspiring and experienced poets to up their game. Poetry is a serious form of play, but it should not be taken too seriously. Once the playfulness gets lost, the fun goes away. The music of language becomes fogged with hierarchies of all kinds, and, quite often, the well goes dry. These materials are directed toward the mature student who can critique his or her own poems.

It is my sincere hope that the thoughts, remarks, and exercises offered here may help poets to value their own hard-won words, despite the fact that their work remains undervalued by the society in which it seems, nonetheless, to thrive.

1. Letting Go & Getting On

"It is well to keep in touch with chaos."

"Poetry is an act of mischief."

—Theodore Roethke

The Writing Life: Letting Go

The weighty matter of *subject* matter seems always to hang in the balance for poets. Do we choose our subject, or does our subject matter choose us? Do we choose where we are going, or do we need to let go and let it take us where it wants to go?

Editor Jim Bodeen, of *Blue Begonia Press*, first posed this question to me. I was confused by that conundrum for nearly a year—*who* or *what* dictates subject matter at any given time—turning it over, and over, in my head.

Indeed, in the poems I was working on during a recent residency I thought I was writing about time. In the privacy of my mind a whole sequence of poems was coming together—though only one had yet been written—like a deck of cards being shuffled in slow motion. A magician holds a deck of cards; makes them into a perfect fan; asks me to pick one card, memorize it, return it.

The card I had memorized was "Temporal Studies." It had the term "Schrödinger's Cat" puzzled into the design on the back of the deck, and, on the face of a few cards sat vague notions of physics concepts I learned as the child of a solar physicist through osmosis. The problem is, I don't know a wit about physics or math. Or, for that matter, about relativity. In a file sat other possible poem titles: *The Always, The Instant, The Hour, The Once.*

But back at home, sitting at my desk, I realized time wasn't really my "subject matter." Perhaps, I came to discover, I was really trying to write about something else. Perhaps Narcissus. I had printed out some preliminary "takes" on Narcissus. I attempted to explain this in a reply to an editor:

> The myth/archetype of drowning (suicide) for love of self seems ripe for exploration. I'm also trying to write about altruism vs. sacrifice and the fine line between the two, as in war... I've written a few pieces so far, and hope also to bring in the Greek and Roman myths as appropriations/mirrors for one another.

> These images will hopefully weave through what I picture as a long poem: mirrors, water, glass, the muses, marble, Paris, Narcissus, and other characters from myths of both ancient cultures: Jupiter, Venus, Daphne, and the feminine models for beauty — Aphrodite, Helen Psyche, Venus, Greek versions vs. their Roman counterparts. I'll be doing "soft" research (so named by David Kirby) rather than encyclopedic work.

> I'm hoping the sacrifice mode/medium might lend itself to some political, albeit subtle, discussions of war and my total bafflement about war will abate, since obviously it's been w/ the human race since the beginning and will, most likely, be our endgame...

A week later, I had written nothing whatsoever about Narcissus, though I had started a file which contained a poem about Rome, and the first line was "Rome, you bastard..." It was indeed a horrible start for a would-be poem.

With only one stanza in the hopper, I remembered Bodeen's koan. *Do we, as poets, choose our subject, or does our subject matter choose us?* It made me uncomfortable once again. I'd felt the muse had been rather stingy while I was creating my poems about time. I was on track, yes. I was writing between ten and twenty pages a day; but frankly, were they worth working on as poems? I suspected the answer was a vehement *no*, even as I wished it were yes.

It came to me—through discomfort, through that question asked by my editor— that there wasn't a place for outlines in poetry. Why, anyway, did I care so much about rounding out the notion of my "current work" with long-range, over-arching statements of thematic purpose? Wouldn't it be better to simply offer myself up, in sacrificial form, arms spread-eagled over the dais, or, with a bent knee and a begging bowl, as a dear friend once said she had, asking God to give her a poem after a particularly dry spell.

Would it be so bad not to write for a few weeks, to

get to the point where I felt so driven I had to write or else I could not sleep, as was my recurrent state for the two decades from 1980–2000, while raising three children? What sharp teeth this muse possessed, and how little s/he cared for my physical, emotional, and mental welfare. But perhaps this was a lesson I needed to learn, and learn again. It was Bodeen, who, in seeing before him the persona of the *Poet*—i.e., a poet with the smugness of finding a cause worthy of writing and then going about the business of writing a manuscript around that cause—detected a lack of honesty.

His query ultimately reveals the chink in the armor of a writer's life built on the pretensions of "going about the business of verse-writing," rather than allowing, or remaining open to one's passions; those obsessions that might lead a writer toward original verse that wants to be written.

It followed that there must be more to the problem of discovering one's subject matter than encyclopedic research, tangential flashes of light sent out from the one of the nine muses, or the mood of one's personal *juju* bag. There must be more to the writer's vocation than a simple desire to avoid a case of writer's block. To get at the gist of things—*no ideas but in things*—a writer must allow him or herself the privilege of exploring those images, issues, and ideas that appeal to the writer's own sensibilities. As Richard Hugo noted, in *The Triggering Town*,

> "It doesn't bother me that the word "stone" appears more than thirty times in my third book, or that "wind" and "gray" appear over and over in my poems to the disdain of some reviewers. If I didn't use them that often I'd be lying about my feelings, and I consider that unforgivable" (p. 15.)

In fact, it is precisely this exploration of those words, memories, sensory and other forms of images that may dictate most clearly the direction for new work. In paying attention to what one is drawn to, the writer comes closer to the elusive nature of association; the subconscious, Jungian archetypes; and all manner of "good stuff," for lack of a better term, that leads to a strong poem.

Perhaps, in the end, the best we can do as writers is to play the game—a variation on hide and seek—we learned as children: Warmer/Colder. Most of us can remember looking for an object in the house or the yard. The lucky one who hid the desirable object would offer clues in the form of "warmer, warmer, no—cold, colder..." The willing victim would stop in her tracks, back step, and wait to hear the words again: "Warm, warmer, aha, warmer—hot, hotter, hottest..." Until you would lay your hands on the buried treasure and say, "Got it."

A Guide for Breaking Lines in Verse

Here are a few general rules to make the process of shaping poems on the page less mysterious. Because poems are confusing enough in and of themselves, anything the writer can do to clarify a poem will help your reader understand it. This is especially important if your poems use figurative language, including metaphors and extended metaphors. An extended metaphor may be referred to as a "conceit." Following a few rules allows the reader to take his or her own "leaps," and to use the imagination, while keeping the literal level of your work intact.

Remember that these guidelines are only suggestions. Many established poets have signature ways of breaking lines that violate some or all of these:

1. The space, or breath, at the end of the line lends power to whatever word is there. So avoid breaking lines on prepositions and articles. Prepositions are parts of speech that describe the relationship between words in a sentence. Some of the more common prepositions are: about, above, after, before, despite, except, for, in, of, off, past, since, to, under, with, and without. Articles are words that, combined with nouns, indicate a type of reference. Examples of articles are: a, an, some, the, this, and that.

2. For stanzaic verse, that is, poems broken into parts with an equal number of lines, generally use beats per line to determine the end words. A beat consists of an "iamb," which resembles a heart beat (da-DA.) Reading aloud can assist you in counting how many beats there are. Half of a beat is sometimes referred to as a "foot." It can also be helpful to count syllables.

3. Be aware of sound in language. There are various ways to become more "musical" while using the English language, and one of these is to read your poems aloud. As you read, listen for masculine vs. feminine line endings. In actuality, the terms "masculine ending" and "feminine ending" are not based on any cultural concept of "masculinity" or "femininity." These terms originate in French grammar, where words of feminine grammatical gender typically end in a *stressless* syllable and words of masculine gender end in a *stressed* syllable. In short, a masculine ending is a stressed syllable that ends a line of verse. For more, see *The New Princeton Encyclopedia of Poetry and Poetics.*

4. To assist your reading the poem in progress, listen to your own breathing. Are the breaths you

take falling on your line breaks? If not, change the line break simply by changing its location.

5. Another way to go about re-lining a piece is to consider the line break as silence, or the musical symbol for "rest." This can be revealing. Without a rest, the music of language gets lost. Words, like a melody, require careful timing. While line breaks alone may seem sufficient, there are cases where the addition of white space can allow a reader more breathing room.

6. Adjectives are tricky. Because they modify nouns, some poets feel that they belong with the noun, and I would agree. Others like to stand an adjective at the end of the line. But because the end word of a line, stanza, or poem is as much or more a position of power as the beginning, I prefer using a stronger word at the end of the line. And, of course, you'll want to pay particular attention to the ending line of your poem—that place of utmost emphasis.

7. While this guideline is ancillary to actually breaking a line, remain consistent in your use of pronouns, tense, and subject/verb agreement. The good news is that these kinds of technical errors are the easiest to fix in a workshop, by

reading your poem aloud, or asking for peer review. If you are unsure about grammar and/or syntax, Strunk & White's classic *The Elements of Style* is a quick read as well as a helpful guide.

8. Finally, remember, rules are made to be broken. There may be cases where the rules simply don't apply. Once you've written a first draft, you become the editor.

Free Verse—Is It Really Free?

Although free verse requires no meter, rhyme, or other traditional techniques, a poet can still use some aspects of form to create structure. In fact, it behooves the writer of poems to strive for some kind of organization. T.S. Eliot wrote "No verse is free for the (man or woman) who wants to do a good job.

Put another way, although free verse requires no meter, rhyme, or other traditional techniques, a poet can still use some aspects of form to create structure. In fact, it behooves a writer of poems to strive for some kind of organization. This is where two time-honored rules of thumb regarding making a successful poem—"Show, don't tell," and "No ideas but in things" come into play.

The first comes to us from Chekhov, the second is from a poem by William Carlos Williams.

Why have these rules been so widely adopted by writers and poets? Perhaps it is because the pitfalls most common to writing poems are editorializing and using abstractions. The tendency to editorialize stems from conversation; it's not surprising that colloquial language enters into a poem. What is difficult is noticing when it does. The need to use an umbrella term rather than an image is also a consequence of our medium as poets. We use language. But if, instead of specific sensory imagery, we choose words such as "hope" and "love," we can trick ourselves into thinking we've conveyed feeling in words when really all we have done is to tell about a feeling. It's the conveyance that matters. To do this requires that language be heightened, concise, original, precise, sensory, and unique, which is another way of saying one must develop a voice.

Of course there are exceptions—Emily Dickinson's famous line "Hope is the thing with feathers" becomes the quintessential breaking of a rule. And, as with any rules, these must be used with caution.

Simple Forms for Free Verse

Because a writer cannot really detach from what he or she has written, take some time to let your poem sit. This might be a day, a week, a month, a year, or a decade. Time is really immaterial in the creative life. What is important is that when you return to the drawing board, you take the time to "mess around" with the work. One way is to use stanzas. Doing so requires that you break your lines in different places, for one thing, and that you cut material if there happens to be a line or two left over after you've divied up the piece into a set number of stanzas of a given length.

It is in this spirit that the following suggestions are offered. Forms that free verse can take include couplets, tercets, and quatrains. Examples by a few poets follow. Granted, many poets working today choose to use formal verse and get around the "problem" of full rhyme with a slant or half rhyme. For many, however, it's enough to vary stanza lengths, which is the function of the couplet—a poem broken into the two line stanzas, the tercet—a poem broken into three line stanzas, and the quatrain, a poem broken into four line stanzas.

Let's begin with a poem written by a poet about her own origins. This choice of subject matter drives home the point "write what you know."

And What Did You Come For?

To hear my name
in the old language,
the endearments of another age.

To see steep-sided mountains.
To learn the many names
for glaciers, *geysirs* and water falling.

To read in dim light the *Sagas*,
the *Eddas*, sung by the *skalds*,
ancient Vikings who before battle

sharpened both blade and tongue,
who halted fighting,
cleaving heads from bodies,

to recite a verse in honor
of the event, their pride
resting on their kenning, their wit.

To touch the drift-backed books,
gut-strung and skin-thick,
vine-twined capitals,

with painted portraits,
the monk's hand copying
word by word on to vellum

by candlelight that guttered
and burned, his body bent
and heartworn, his fingers

cramping in the damp,
his fingers reaching out
through time to mine.

—Sigrun Susan Lane

This poem uses tercets. Once you have completed a first or second draft of a piece, the use of stanzas in a certain set of lines may become a means of winnowing out little word padding. It allows you to see and hear (read aloud) where the voice changes. Has showing given way to telling? Has the persona in the poem begun to editorialize or over-explain? When you find such places, simply eliminate them, do the math, and see whether your piece wants to fall naturally into couplets, tercets, or quatrains.

You can, gratis your word processor, change drafts very quickly, take out words, and re-line your piece. Be sure to keep subsequent versions, as one of the pitfalls of this kind of revision is overwork. Just as an artist can ruin a canvas by going over it one too many times, a poet can ruin a poem. Ultimately, by virtue of its lack of predetermined form, a free verse poem has the potential to take on a unique shape. When s/he uses free verse, the poet possesses more license to express his or her particularities, as well as more control over development and shape. The results can be dazzling:

Light Years

Is light the last thing lost or never lost at all?
There is light so far away, it's gone

by the time we see it,
the tail lights on the highway far ahead

that say someone is traveling
this same dark way.

Those blue clumps lost ten billion light
years ago at the edge of the universe

redshift from ultraviolet to the visible
and are found by the Hubble telescope,

sleek horse pulling through dark
the reeling carriages of space

even as they change into roses
or thunderheads or phantom animals

we never imagined.
What fiery dust was our beginning,

left us a tender earth? Far out in the universe
a tomorrow we can't see is singing the last word

of a song we heard long ago under stars
like blossoms on black water.

—Joan Swift, *The Atlantic*

Requiem for Agamemnon

At first no crime was committed, just a sibylline
voice moving the clock fingers. I played for tension,
percussed the drumbeat of your chest.

Your heart improvised, voted for choppy rhythms,
tightened each string, easing off before it broke.
My fingers pressed against your skin, unable to read

the ballad. I swallowed the story whole, took a spoke
of sunlight and hammered it into the thin metal mask
of your face. My tongue protested to an empty room.

No one believed my prophecy. You sang the same requiem,
over and over, without knowing it was your own.
Every word cut deeply. I harmonized, but could not rescue

you from yourself. Take my hand and trace each wrinkle,
measure the blows. I tell you hunger is not my problem,
only this endless scraping of knife against bone.

—Sharon Carter

The Skeletons of Man and Dog Embrace

—"Written in Bone," Exhibit on Forensic Skeletal Research,
Museum of Natural History, Washington DC 2013

"Being dead never hurt anybody."
Neither did being sent to the body farm,
so scientists could study his corpse's decay
before shipping the museum the remaining remains.

This was all as he wanted it.
"I've been a teacher all my life
and I think I might as well be a teacher
after I'm dead, so why don't I just give you my body?"

There was a catch: three Irish wolfhounds
came with the package, skeletons pre-cleaned
by burial under his lawn, where they'd shared space
with a lion. Never a dull moment in osteology, or cryptozoology,

the study of animals whose existence
is unproven. One of the "Four Horseman
of Sasquatchery," he irked his peers by exploring the hints
around the idea of Bigfoot, lived/died in hope of seeing one,

though advocated shooting it on sight.
"I wouldn't want a live one captured," he said.
"That would be the cruelest thing I can imagine.
Shoot one. Criminy. Being dead never hurt anybody."

He dropped the Dead Sea Scrolls
on his toe and broke it, married Einstein's granddaughter,
and may have learned more about love from a 160-pound dog
than from four wives. Through it all, he had kept all his baby teeth.

They were in the box from the body farm,
with the dogs' bones. The Smithsonian sculptor
had to match the pieces to a picture of a hug between Grover,
6-foot-3, and Clyde, seven foot, four legs. "It was like a jigsaw puzzle,"

the artist said. "But it was like putting two
together at the same time and having them meet
somewhere in the middle," as Krantz had wanted to encounter
Big Foot, cross-species, and hoped to reach out to us, from beyond.

                                        —Tina Kelley

Enjambment: The Ragged Line

Enjambment—the continuation of a sentence or clause across a line-break—is an indispensable tool, one particularly useful for breaking lines in unexpected places to create the element of surprise or suspense:

> "If a poet allows all the sentences of a poem to end in the same place as regular line-breaks, a kind of deadening can happen in the ear, and in the brain too, as all the thoughts can end up being the same length. Enjambment is one way of creating audible interest..." (*The Poetry Archive,* paragraph 1.)

It is not only the interest created by enjambment that leads a writer of poems toward this device. For free verse, both enjambment and the caesura are two methods of variation one can employ without turning toward formal methods. As Robert Frost famously noted, it is difficult to play tennis without a net. Yet it takes only remarkably simple changes in style to create a framework on which to "hang" one's words. As an added bonus, quite often writer's block may give way to a simple change in style.

So if you have just a few lines of material, or a bare bones idea, writing in a form that could be called "The Ragged Line" may help you to round your subject matter out. Think of it as play. After a few drafts, if you let the lines break such that there is a more structural form to the piece, and you may discover your poem hiding beneath its words.

A few examples of poems using enjambment follow. Certainly it's not an overstatement to say that enjambment can become indispensable to the poet working in free or open verse. It's also a tool formal poets use to good effect.

The Dark That in the Hemlock Hides

Turns
     its clock-face
toward me.
Wrapped in the cloak
     of its night
hunt,
the barred
     feathers
   disappear
against bark.
     In its own
  time, black-lit chars
     of eyes
see what they see,
say what they
     say.
For years,
I have sought to pry from
     the disguise
of different species
     some
portent, passion,
    Psalm.

The calm
          face stays
                    closed. Today,
          below the cove
                    of red-twigged
dogwood
          a spotted
bellied towhee
                    sighs
its two-note
          —Not now.

                    —Pamela Gross

Man Staggering, Bronze

Giacometti

Now this tipped
off-kilter figure, head
thrown back, arm
thrust out to catch himself.
A futile gesture. Barely attached
to the base, his form
a metaphor for falling, he is—
not captured—flung
into being at the moment
before all is lost, the moment
all will certainly be lost, I think,
a brave moment.
How does he not
clang to the floor, his ropy length

and metal weight not
bring him down, not finish
but suspend his tilt
toward the absence
his arabesque embraces.

—Anne Pitkin

The Caesura

The term "caesura" means a complete pause in a line
of poetry, or in music. The plural form of *caesura* is
caesurae. Another way to define this term is a pause in
a line determined by the natural rhythm of the diction.
In Frost's famous poem "The Road Not Taken," the line
"Two roads diverged // in a yellow wood" holds a natural
caesura. Finally, it can be said that a caesura is a mid-
line stop, for example:

MACBETH

If it were done when 'tis done; then twere well
It were done quickly. If that assassination
Could trammel up the consequence...

The caesura occurs between "quickly" and "if—
note the full stop in the middle, rather than at the end
of the line. These full stops can be found throughout

Shakespeare, Gilgamesh, early Anglo-Saxon poetry and verse sagas (e.g. Beowulf). Because contemporary poets likewise seek music and meaning, the caesura functions to give a reader, or a listener, time to absorb words and images.

Equally important, adding some breathing room to a line slows the reader down. Because the goal of a poem is to compress and heighten language, white space can hardly be over-rated. The use of a form such as the caesura may not necessarily come into play during first drafts or free-writes, when structure on the page is not nearly as important as content. But breaking a line in half can be used to the poet's advantage during subsequent revisions. In the piece below by Roberta Feins, it highlights verbs unique to weaving:

The River Tarn at Albi

Wind threshes beats the clouds
    with bladed shingle.

Combs of church steeples hackle streams
    of rain drawn plied spun

on the Mother-of-All wheel of the old bridge
    her piers a loom heddle separating warp

of gray waters turning the ratchet.
    Shafts of plumed herons

treadle the reedy bank great carp
    with pinecone scales fluttering,

shoot through the shed of braided silver
    weave a splendid brocade tapestry.

—Roberta Feins

Finally, to show that play is always "at play" in poetry, Lynn Emanuel goes so far as to use triple caesuras per line in her poem "She," which is typeset horizontally on the page in her award-winning book *Then, Suddenly*.

An Interview with Jeremy Voigt

Jeremy Voigt: The natural world seems to play a major role in your writing. Do you see yourself as a nature poet, a regional poet, or a poet of any particular place?

Judith Skillman: I guess I would prefer not to be labeled as any particular kind of poet, other than, perhaps, someone who loves to write about what happens inside and outside the self. Nothing seems too small to be worth writing about, or too big. I do love nature but I am not a "nature girl," since I depend upon white noise in order to sleep and have rituals that are dangerously obsessive compulsive. Having said that, I am so glad I moved to Washington State from Maryland in 1982. The northwest is my landscape. I've lived here for twenty-six years now, which is longer than I ever lived in upstate New York or Maryland. I love the light here, the terrain, the flora and fauna. I love that there is no poison ivy! And I also feel Washington State is unique for the way we can go over the pass and find ourselves in an entirely different kind of landscape within an hour.

JV: Could you talk a bit about your specific writing process?

JS: I don't follow a schedule, as my life is too hectic, much like everyone's these days. But I do try to be receptive to the muse, or "inspiration." If it has been a week and I've not been applying the seat of pants to the seat of the chair--to use a fiction-writing maxim--I do sit down to write. Taking walks is more of a luxury than it used to be, but walking definitely helps generate the kind of thoughts that lead to poem writing, if not poems. So does any activity outside, like gardening, hiking, or star gazing. Sometimes a title or a line will come to me, and while I don't carry a notebook, and I don't journal as many writers do, I pay particular attention to words that come out of nowhere. The exception to this rule might be words that occur in a dream (yes, I do speak in my sleep) which often, while seeming profound during "dreamtime" amount to nothing more than "Hand me the handle."

I try to have more than one iron in the fire, and when I am stuck, I go back and revise older work. I also use revision to "jump start" the writing process when I feel dry or "used up," and try to keep reading and learning from other writers as much as time allows.

Having birthed and brought up three children, I thrive on interruption. Mothering teaches humility, and the interruption factor is perhaps the most lasting lesson. I used to think it was horrible; now I rather crave it. I know taking breaks from a poem often allows clarity to enter the scene, and also takes pressure off the angst of trying too hard.

JV: In the introduction to "Heat Lightning" David Kirby mentions the range of your work—from poems that use conversational language to poems that might be classified as "language" poetry. Do you see yourself as fitting within a particular poetics?

JS: I suppose if I were to categorize my verse writing, it would fit within free/open verse, but free verse with constraints. I have written formal verse—including sonnets, sestinas, pantoums, and blank verse. In addition, I have dabbled in concrete and structural verse. But I am more interested in pursuing the associative process while writing. This becomes more difficult when constraints are placed on any element used in verse writing: the sound, sense, or visual format of the English language.

I think a worthwhile goal is to remain open to content and to write using whatever kind of form best fits each poem's particular, specific nature with regard to its subject matter. Let content/subject matter becomes the raison d'être. The pull toward a subject is highly subjective and may encompass the contemporary landscape, the problems of relationships, the beauty of nature, or metaphysics. I try to avoid overt politics, as corruption doesn't lend itself to the explorative process of poem-making.

Two constraints I've found particularly useful are counting the number of beats per line, and the number of lines per stanza. When using a set stanza and/or number of beats as a measuring device, a poem sometimes will fall into a more "minimalist" structure, and this is something I do strive for-- lyrics that aren't over-wordy, poems that resist the little word padding of language. These words are necessary as connective tissue in prose; in poetry they can ruin a good line. The poem's content drives the form.

JV: "Prisoner of the Swifts" is a provocative title. Could you talk a bit about your new manuscript?

JS: My new manuscript deals with the loss of the pastoral, endangered species, antiques, and the general malaise of this 21st century. Poems such as "Losing the Hurry,"--written, incidentally, at Centrum--speak to a sense of time moving in slow motion, as it used to, and how the loss of that kind of time impacts one's relationship to nature.

The title poem was written in March of this year, when a flock of swifts quite literally took over our house and yard. We felt as if the blue angels were flying around us. When I looked into the species--I like to do "loose" research for some poems--I discovered that swifts only land on vertical surfaces. They mate in the air and never touch down at all. They are also the fastest flyers in the bird kingdom. I did feel imprisoned by them in the two weeks they adopted our yard as their territory. As I worked on that piece, the extended metaphor for the manuscript morphed from the guilt response and reverse victimization that accompanies our defilement of planet earth, to a perhaps more "nuanced" version: despite the human/inhumane imperatives to take over our myriad underlings, nature will win out, one way or another.

JV: David Kirby also mentions, in his introduction to

"Heat Lightning," your use of humor in combination with or in contrast to strong emotional content. What role do you see humor playing in your writing?

JS: I feel that humor is a by-product of particular poems at times, but it is not a thing I strive for. In fact, most of my poems are not funny whatsoever, though sometimes while work-shopping them I find my colleagues react to lines as though they are funny in a film noir kind of way. It troubles me that within the last two decades poets have had to worry about "entertaining" the audience. I realize that poetry can be very dull, and sometimes overly serious. I don't think there is any way to set out writing the comedic poem in order to entertain a crowd while at the same time trying to find one's uniquely physical presence, place in space/time, and emotionally charged territory. The latter is the place I prefer to be, by far.

JV: What writers would you name as having major influence in your writing?

JS: I began reading poems in high school by Diane Wakowski and by Japanese poets translated into English and from there into undergraduate work I read Eliot, Berryman, Coleridge, Keats, Shakespeare, et al. I was lucky to attend the University of Maryland, which had an excellent reading series, and got to hear

Tess Gallagher way back in 1975, as well as Galway Kinnell, Stanley Kunitz, and other contemporary poets. In my reading over the past three decades I have gone through lots of stages. Like a fad or an affair I would take up with James Wright or Patianne Rogers for a year and not read anyone else. In the past decade I've come to love Philip Levine, Czeslaw Milosz, and Jack Gilbert. I return to their books, now dog-eared. I especially enjoy reading translations of Tomas Tranströmer, Friedrich Hölderlin, Fernando Pessoa, Pablo Neruda, Paul Celan, Cesar Vallejo, Edith Södergran, and many others. Recently at a bookstore in Half Moon Bay (south of SF) I came across a treasure: Herman Hesse's "Poems" translated by James Wright.

JV: Humor seems to be a popular mode at the moment. Do you see this as a positive trend in the poetry world? I concur with Kirby as it seems to me that your use of humor is often a counter point to dark or powerful subjects. For example in "The Librarian Decides on Cryonics" the poem seems to move as a lament to the loss of reading culture as the librarian's head is "stuffed with children's books / and the thin yellow cards of the catalogue," then the poem turns into an elegy and its major subject which is death and legacy, "the slim volumes filled with their choices: / die or be frozen, freeze-dried."

JS: Well, the popularity of humor in poetry disturbs me, as I mentioned. I am not sure why it has become such a trend. I had no idea, at the time of writing "The Librarian" that this would be a funny piece, or an entertaining one. It is quite dated now. I'd say that humor has its uses in society and therefore it can be a diffuser of anxiety in literature as well. But, ultimately, the associative element of language is what I like best about poems. A well-wrought poem is like a dream—all kinds of stuff combines to make the piece come off right, but there isn't always an analytic or rational way of understanding how the disparate elements work together for the larger whole or extended metaphor.

I should say that I do like narrative verse as well, especially when it is forcefully combined with imagery as Philip Levine's work, but I love the lyrical bent of Jack Gilbert at his most deadly serious, and likewise all the "Great American Poets," including Bishop, Williams, Frost, Plath, Stevens, Pound, et al.

JV: I recall reading somewhere that Aristotle called metaphor a "mistake of the mind." How does association play a specific role in your process of writing a poem? Is it present in certain stages of the writing process or pervasive?

JS: Association and the associative process is definitely at the heart of my own writing. I try to write when I feel rather foggy about things. "Mystical" might be to pat a word to use, but remaining open to the bizarre sounds even worse. As Richard Hugo, said, "The imagination is a cynic." If metaphor is a "mistake of the mind," it's good that the mind can also be allowed to make mistakes. Ultimately, we are not aware of what goes on below the tip of the iceberg. Our conscious, waking, functional state of mind, the specialists now say, comprises only ten percent of the brain. So it's more than a bit fun to allow the mind to have its say on things, and that includes a willful suspension of disbelief.

Perhaps those monsters, demons, feverish hallucinations and nightmarish creations we experienced as young children can remain with us throughout our lives, if we recognize them for what they are. To bring the subconscious into play is a powerful and scary thing to do, but our subconscious has much to say, and it can be a friend and partner with us in our lives if we allow it to come out of hiding, albeit only occasionally.

JV: Reginald Sheppard wrote an interesting article in the summer edition of the Writer's Chronicle where he argues in favor of difficulty in poetry. This seems counter to popular trends, though not necessarily totally counter to publishing trends (it seems to me that much of poetry published currently is difficult in a good way). Your poems are often rooted in clear domestic or natural images, but seem to resist mere description in favor of pursuing something more abstract (a thing that may not be clear to the reader or the speaker of the poem). I'm thinking of poems like "Magpie Eyes." I wonder if you have any thoughts about current trends of difficulty in poetry (or the resistance to it) in current contemporary poetry?

JS: I think there has always been a resistance to difficulty in language, and the English language is no different. The poem is the perfect place, however, to allow things to be difficult. This goes back to the nature of the subconscious and the complex human psyche. It would be wrong to inject simplicity and accessibility into poetry, when humans are in no way simple. Our lives begin and end alone; our emotions encompass paradoxical worlds. Human beings are like mysterious magnets. Poems should not pretend to be otherwise.

What seems to be happening now is that the difficulty inherent in words as symbols of things has been overtaken, or eclipsed by, the kind of poetry that exacts difficulty from the placement and syntax of the words themselves. I see this as a bad thing for poetry in general, and a sad situation for poets, especially.

Once we get caught up in syntax, if we are not e e cummings, and we are not, we may get lost on the page. So many poets seem to be doing back handsprings in order to pull off original verse, but the more gymnastics they do, the less meaning there is in the work. This goes right back to the importance of subject matter. Content is everything. Form must follow content. It seems to me there is no reason to take language, which is an inherently difficult venue for the expression of art, and make it more difficult for the sake of impressing a reader. The best poems are those that go through you like a bullet train. They are made of words and plain English, but they leave you wondering what went by.

Poetry Vs. Prose

Let's dive right in:

Poetry

Ladislaw the critic
is five feet six inches high,
which means
that his eyes
are five feet two inches
from the ground,
which means,
if you read him your poem,
and his eyes lift to five feet
and a trifle more than two inches,
what you have done
is Poetry—
should his eyes remain

at five feet two inches,
you have perpetrated prose,
and do his eyes stoop
--which Heaven forbid!—
the least trifle below
five feet two inches,
you
are an unspeakable adjective.

—Alfred Kreymborg

Read Ladislaw your poem. Have you "perpetrated prose"—which must be a venial sin? Don't beat yourself up—instead, ask yourself what really distinguishes poetry from prose? While you're at it, ask a few other questions. Is the prose poem a poem? And why is it the worst thing, in the downward glancing eyes of this Czech King, to be "an unspeakable adjective"?

Poetry is unique in that the impact of every single word counts. To discover your own obsessions becomes not only desirable but necessary. The subject matter that attracts you will be your best subject. It seems, on the face of it, quite simple. But how do you learn to trust your own instincts, when society, and school, in particular, has spent a number of years, training you to conform and ignore the internal signals that govern your original, voice? This begins when you start listening and paying attention to your thoughts. Of course we all know that self-talk "should" be positive. Not so much, though, for the purpose of writing poems.

For writing requires the kind of honesty that might be termed "gentle," "nurturing," and "available." It requires you to stop and take the time to reflect upon memories and events, something you may feel you have no time for. It is, however, your own particular array of sensory experience, imagery, dream-like associations, and, yes, dreams, that yield originality. Find out what time of day you feel most comfortable exploring these things, and set aside some time. It doesn't have to be every day. But it does have to be the right time of day or night.

Once you begin a piece, don't forget to include your body—the five senses, the parts of yourself that can role-play, and don't be afraid to think of yourself as somebody else. This capacity is essential not only to empathy, but to negative capability, that much-touted phrase coined by Keats, that speaks to the capacity of human beings to transcend and revise their contexts. It's essential not to confuse the persona in a poem with the person writing the poem. A persona is simply the character assumed by an author in a written work; it is not and never will be that author.

To return to Kreymborg's poem, then, a certain confidence of voice is one of the things required in order to not offend Ladislaw the critic. It follows that to assert one's own will and individuality upon one's subject matter is not only desirable, it is required. There's no other way to get from the images and sounds to that sixth sense, the gestalt that comes from combining, in a sophisticated yet uniquely personal fashion, the disparate elements that go into making a poem successful.

Finally, if you find that you have a string of adjectives, or even two in a row, choose the best one. The strongest words are verbs. Adjectives can be helpful, but they can also become unwieldy. Strip out your language, and cultivate associative writing, which is a private or personal kind of writing—a text composed for oneself. Don't think about your audience, the audience, any audience. Your task is to confront your subject matter head on. As an equestrian instructor once said, "Look where you're going and go where you're looking."

The task of learning to write associatively, and therefore, interestingly—enough to lift Ladislaw's eyes "a trifle"— becomes a life-long drive to enhance imagery, to go for the music inherent in language. It is the working of one's own verbal thought into patterns and arrangements that may create unpleasant emotion, but may also assist the writer in discerning some structure beneath experience. If at all possible, write at a time when you are close to your dreams. That is, when you first wake up, or before you turn in.

The Fine Art of Revision

There are two aspects to the revising process: technique and content. I'm going to focus more, here, on content, as that is the part of the process that is most often given short shrift, while style, technique and grammar get the lion's share of attention.

Style can be covered relatively quickly by keeping a few guidelines in mind. Never confuse your reader unnecessarily by misusing punctuation, verb tenses, subject/verb agreement, and confusing pronoun references. Strunk & White's guide *The Elements of Style* is a quick read and ever-ready reference for any writer. The poem, if it is to succeed, must do so on its merits, not by reliance on artificial devices or tricks. The rule of thumb here is never confuse your reader unnecessarily by language usage. Poems can be confusing enough.

While perusing these suggestions for in-depth revision, feel free to take what you like and leave the rest. Revision is an individual process; what works for one poet doesn't work for another. It is only by trial and error that we find the tools to allow us to deepen our poems and continue our personal growth in the art and craft of verse writing.

There are many ways you can revise your poem for content. Think of a poem as a room in a house. When remodeling a room there are many options. One can choose any from any number of possibilities from rearranging the furniture, to painting a wall, adding built-in shelving, to pushing out one part of the exterior to create additional space. Even a simple touch, such as replacing that faded mock-Persian rug with a brighter carpet, or a patterned piece, makes a difference. The scope of choices for revising each and every piece we write becomes an unlimited palette when we remain open.

It's important not to view any particular version of a piece as "finished." Rather, keep your mind open to the assortment of choices for revision, which are limitless. Write, write again; work, re-work. Ultimately, as you refine and polish your poem, you will find the gist of the piece. It may be quite different than where you thought you were headed when you started out.

SUGGESTIONS FOR IN-DEPTH REVISION:

- Select the one line that you feel has the most energy, and begin another poem with that line. To quote Roethke: "The problem is to seize upon what is worth preserving in immature work—the single phrase of real poetry, the line that has energy--and to build it into a complete piece that has its own shape and motion."

- Re-write the poem from another point of view, either personal ("I", "We"); imperative ("You"); or objective ("He," "She," "It," "One," "They").

- Change the stanza lengths to a set number, if the poem is blocky or has no stanza breaks, or if the stanzas seem arbitrary. To do this, read the poem aloud and listen for natural pauses in the piece. Then re-write the poem in these set stanzas. Or you may wish to take the stanza breaks out and write another version using different stanza lengths. As you do this, you will need to cut out "little word padding." This approach has an added advantage: paring down inevitably strengthens the language of your poem.

- Choose a number of beats per line--anything from dimeter (two beats) to iambic pentameter (five beats, the standard for a sonnet or other formal poetry such as blank/formal verse.) Rewrite the poem, beginning with the stanza or line you feel is strongest.

- If you handwrite your work, turn your paper the long way and write in long lines using the entire length of the page.

- Try breaking the poem into pieces separated by asterisks, a la "Thirteen Ways of Looking at a Blackbird," by Wallace Stevens. As you write, think of your poem as if you were a stranger moving around the subject matter and staring in at it from various windows of "the room," or "house,"—that metaphoric place in which the poem takes place.

- Switch tenses. If the poem is in the present tense, rewrite it in the past. Or stage the poem in the future. Then, using what works and isn't too awkward, go back to the original version and decide what tense your poem really "wants" to be in.

- "Implode" your poem. If it is thirty lines, try cutting it back to five. You may choose to use the proportion of one-sixth length, or choose another. You can make a haiku from a page-length poem, and then use this "seed poem" to help you develop the gist of your original poem.

- "Explode" your poem. Use the form of a "Glosa" ("...In its strict form it is a poem consisting of a line or short stanza...stating the theme of the poem, and followed by one stanza for each line of the (first/main stanza,) explaining or glossing that line..." *Princeton Encyclopedia of Poetry and Poetics*) to develop and lengthen the poem, while expanding your meaning and working to develop the extended metaphor(s) inherent in your material.

- Make an assumption, a la Richard Hugo, and incorporate this assumption into the poem as you revise. See Chapter 3 of *The Triggering Town*: "Assumptions lie behind the work of most writers. The writer is unaware of most of them, and most of them are weird. Often the weirder the better..." (Hugo, 19)

- According to William Stafford, "...vagueness (is) necessary for art...Writers have many things to be careful not to know, and strangely, one of the things not to know is how to write. Sometimes writers who have wandered into good poems have become too adept..." (Stafford, 66). Rewrite your poem, striving for this vague, not-knowing quality. In other words, if you are certain where the poem is going, take some detours along the way, and you may find that the poem desires to go to another place. Remain open to surprises as you revise.

● A certain amount of angst is endemic to the writer's vocation. Too much anxiety can be crippling, however. It's helpful to remember what Ernest Hemingway said in an interview about his own writing. This excerpt is taken from "Working Habits": "How can you learn not to worry?" "By not thinking about it. As soon as you start to think about it, stop it. Think about something else. You have to learn that."

2. Giving Writer's Block the Boot

"Pick a subject, writers, equal to your strength and take some time to consider what your shoulders should refuse and what they can bear. Neither eloquence nor clear organization will forsake one who has chosen a subject within his capabilities…"

from Horace's *Ars Poetica*

The Pressure to Write: Can Angst Become a Poem?

Sometimes it is our own, particular reasons for writing that can teach us the most about why we feel pressured to write poems. To put it another way, if we choose to write about why we write, we may not only get an answer and/or relief to the struggle, we may break through the constraints inherent in this art form. And, if we write about why we write in the form of a poem, the result will be the "ars poetica," which basically means "the art of poetry." The definition of this term in contemporary poetics extends to various techniques of rhetoric, including but not limited to: writing about writing, singing about singing, thinking about thinking, etc.

Not surprisingly, then, an "ars poetica" poem can be thought of as that piece of a particular poet's canon that best defines the author's personal theory of writing, as well as encompassing his or her ideals. The "ars poetica" form may be regarded as the quintessential poem, in that it distills and exemplifies essential qualities found in a poet's canon, and therefore lends transparency to an author's signature—his or her style, voice, and choice of formal or informal verse.

Reading and writing these kinds of poems can become a generative force for poetry as well as other creative media. The ars poetica poem is to poetry what the ekphrastic poem is to art—that is one comparison, except that in each case the medium is poetry. The point is, when we use one art to praise another, or, in this case, when we use our writing skills to examine the motivation behind why we are driven to write and what we are doing when we write, important information comes out of the process. Sometimes even enlightenment—an 'aha'!

At the very least, these exercises should assist you in writing more often, and writing in a more condensed and/ or associative and/or experimental fashion: the choice is up to you. You may opt for formal verse, as structure can and does provide inspiration for many contemporary poets.

As you write about why you want to write, continue to view this work as a process. What we strive for is an illumination—that by holding a mirror up to ourselves we might not 'drown' as Narcissus did, but, rather, we might begin to swim. And that is the point. There is so much imagination within each individual. Each poet has a unique set of experiences, language facility, and childhood. So when we begin to draw on these and reflect on the act of writing, it sometimes happens that a voice emerges. You might find yourself wanting to use certain forms or devices. Likewise, or otherwise, you may find you prefer to write in long lines and almost use prose, or the prose poem. Whatever the vehicle may be—that is not the most important thing. What is critical to the process of finding your own voice is to continue peeling back layers of the onion until you get to the heart of the matter, and discover your own unique sensibility and obsessions. You may find a bit of this discovery—your own hidden territory—rubs off on other pieces.

Once you get the hang of it, the ars poetica poem is everywhere, in every poet's canon. Wallace Stevens has written a whole book of them, if you peruse his collected works, *The Palm at the End of the Mind.*

One of the most anthologized poems is Marianne Moore's. From the first line, "I too dislike it,...", Moore immediately disposes of any claim to pomposity, which is one of the problems most readers have in their conceptions of poetry, generally formed from early school experiences, when as students they were forced to memorize arcane, pedantic, full-rhyme poems. Notice Moore's use of indentation, enjambment, and line breaks in this excerpt from her famous work:

Poetry

I, too, dislike it: there are things that are important
beyond all this fiddle.
Reading it, however, with a perfect contempt for it,
one discovers that there is in
it, after all, a place for the genuine.
Hands that can grasp, eyes
that can dilate, hair that can rise

if it must, these things are important not be-
cause a high-sounding interpretation can be put upon them
but because they are
useful. When they become so derivative as to
become unintelligible, the
same thing may be said for all of us—that we
do not admire what
we cannot understand. The bat,
holding on upside down or in quest of some-
thing to

eat, elephants pushing, a wild horse taking a roll,
a tireless wolf under
a tree, the immovable critic twitching his skin like a
horse that feels a flea, the base-
ball fan, the statistician—case after case
could be cited did
one wish it; nor is it valid
to discriminate against "business documents and

school-book"; all these phenomena are important...

(excerpted from *Selected Poems*,
Marianne Moore, 1935)

The benefit of discovering a poet's particular
philosophy (granted, there may be more than one, but
generally one stands out), is not only that a reader can
perceive a distillation, or essential 'theory of poetics'
there, but one may use the poem as a basis for comparison
with other poets. Neruda, for example, is quite clear that
the poet's "art" is more than a merely personal endeavor;

it encapsulates the "obligation" of an artist to society, and does so in the first person. His poem is not playful. While it does not include the whimsical, specific images of Moore's vision, Neruda's poem is not dismissive of poetry's necessary derivatives, which, for him, become intelligible precisely because they speak in natural voices. (see "The Poet's Obligation," page 68)

Although there are many passive attitudes in this poem, which is taken from one of the poet's own personal favorite collections, "Fully Empowered," and written during a particularly fruitful time in the writer's life, the overall sense is one of great activity and depth. The poet as vessel for the sea: "a breaking up of foam and quicksand" (l. 26) responds as one who may pass through normal boundaries of self, cell, prison, building, and window, much as water can flood. The person who receives the gift of 'freedom', however, is almost a communal persona: "...and, hearing me, eyes may lift themselves" (l. 22).

This oblique distancing mechanism has the effect of making the "poet's obligation" not one of egoism and personal power, but rather, a sincere marriage to natural forces. Reading other of Neruda's poems, one experiences the same subtle distancing of the writer's persona from the writer himself. It is this unique ability that contributed to Neruda's profound influence and breadth.

While admiring poets of this ilk, and reading work that attracts and invites us to create, the occupational hazard of writing poetry is not being able to write poetry. Everyone experiences the dreaded "Writer's Block" at some point. Whether the feeling of not being able to do one's work becomes a habit is, however, up to the writer. The trick is to distract yourself from the "not-being-able-to" feelings by turning your attention toward accomplishing a small piece of work. As William Stafford said, "Can't write? Lower your standards."

Jump Start!

The following exercises were designed to allow the writer the latitude to explore his or her self-talk about writing—including the uncomfortable need to write while feeling helpless to begin—through exercises directed toward *writing about writing*. Poets and prose writers have expressed themselves abundantly about both their frustrations and pleasures with the muse. Unless otherwise directed, the choice of form, or lack thereof, is left up to the writer. You can use the form of long lines and/or prose poem (in its simplest terms, a poem without line breaks) for your first draft. Then break the lines as you see fit, if you decide to revise an exercise.

Note: Because these prompts are intended to break through "writer's block" always begin with a free-write. Find a quiet place, set the timer for ten minutes, and don't stop writing until the timer goes off. This requires that you still your inner critic. You can't be writer, and judge, and jury at the same time.

A Note about the Poems

Each of the poems about poetry incorporated into the following exercises addresses fundamental questions regarding the difficulties of writing poems, the issue of a social obligation (or lack thereof), visitations by muses or demons, the singular destiny of the poet, the loneliness of poetry as an art form, and, finally, the potentially destructive possibilities inherent in truth-telling through the vehicle of verse.

As you read the pieces selected to accompany these exercises, consider the questions each persona poses, sometimes playfully, as in Milosz's almost bantering yet academic tone, and Gilbert's stubborn anger at the act of writing. Does the poet owe his gifts to a society, taken as a single person or a community, who may or may not appreciate them? Is the poet in debt to society? Neruda seems to think so. These questions are not vague, though; in Steven's case, they may echo a kind of labyrinth of the imagination.

In any case, reading this work can be a telling experience, especially when one considers the varied canon of each of these writers—from the insurance salesman to the hermetic monk to the communist who left his native Chile to become not only a household name, but a world-renowned speaker on the subject of human rights.

Feel free to try the exercises sequentially, or to select one exercise that appeals to you. And remember, whatever comes from your efforts—whether you use a laptop or a #2 pencil—don't belittle the results. You conquer writer's block once you begin the act of writing.

1: You Have Been Forbidden to Write

For this exercise, imagine that the state, the government, the secret service, Special Forces, FBI, or CIA has expressly forbidden you to write on penalty of going to prison.

Or you are in solitary confinement and have not got anything to write with, not even a bit of charcoal or soap. You may need to use your own blood.

What is it you would give your life to write? This is your last chance. It's midnight. At dawn you face the firing squad.

For the faint of heart: A relative close to you has asked you not to write about them. You are in a comfy chair at Starbucks with a mocha latte, your favorite pen, and notebook paper. Write to or about this relative.

2: Discover Your Process in an Animal

For this free-write, choose an animal for which you feel an affinity. It could be a domesticated animal such as a cat or dog—or a ferret. Or you may choose a creature of the wild, or an animal that has wandered into the suburbs for lack of a habitat. Got the animal? OK, read Brendan Galvin's poem "Ars Poetica: The Foxes," below. Allow your imagination to explore the sensory experience of writing, as Galvin does. Heighten the proximity of the animal by using concrete details.

Ars Poetica: The Foxes

What will make it red as that one
years ago by the woodpile, a fox that loitered
as though in revelation's flames for
a telltale whiff of rodent beneath the snow?
Not these windfall apples hard as cue balls
in the cold, not even that pumpkin I recycled
to its plot as too big and stringy for a pie,
folded now into a white turban. Snow
is on the ground this January dusk,
and this fox, flat black and gray,
no burning bush, walks without hurry

among the fruit trees, then behind the sled,
and is gone. Barely a fox at all, barely more
than a tremor of wind in the bushes
behind the orchard, it needs a tidbit
of cottontail or field mouse, the under-shed
hold outs against January, small
and blooded, to stagger its footprints
too fastidiously placed.

—Brendan Galvin

3: Add Complexity

Read Wallace Stevens "Poetry is a Destructive Force" below. Choose an animal from the wild as you free-write for ten minutes, getting in touch with your own passion for this animal as an analogy to the passion to write. Continue exploring your relationship to poetry through the animal—whether it is a wolf, lion, or one of the many endangered/extinct species on earth—in subsequent drafts.

Poetry Is a Destructive Force

That's what misery is,
Nothing to have at heart.
It is to have or nothing.

It is a thing to have,
A lion, an ox in his breast,
To feel it breathing there.

Corazon, stout dog,
Young ox, bow-legged bear,
He tastes its blood, not spit.

He is like a man
In the body of a violent beast.
Its muscles are his own...

The lion sleeps in the sun.
Its nose is on its paws.
It can kill a man.

—Wallace Stevens

4: Discover Your Process in an Object

For this exercise, choose an object that has a mysterious story behind it—a story only you know, which was handed down to you by your parents and/ or grandparents. Write that story, using concrete details about the object you have chosen.

5: On Trying to Write

Using one or two of Gilbert's poems "Trying to Write Poetry" and "Doing Poetry," below, free-write your own piece about the process of writing poems as you experience it.

Any emotions that come into play are fair game: frustration, exhilaration, boredom, lassitude, depression, agitation, nervousness, writer's block, etc.

Before you begin a first draft, take some time to jot down notes on what you feel are your best works. What circumstances led to the writing? Are your memories of those triggers good or bad? What environment facilitated the work? Were you at home or traveling?

Another way to get to this type of poem might be to consider the difficulties inherent in trying to write poetry (or prose). What is it like for you? What analogy/metaphor might you use for your own process?

Métier

The Greek fisherman do not
play on the beach and I don't
write funny poems.

—Jack Gilbert

Doing Poetry

Poem, you sonofabitch, it's bad enough
that I embarrass myself working so hard
to get it right even a little,
and that little grudging and awkward.
But it's afterwards I resent, when
the sweet sure should hold me like
a trout in the bright summer stream.
There should be at least briefly

access to your glamour and tenderness.
But there's always this same old
dissatisfaction instead.

—Jack Gilbert

6: Write a Short Poem about Writing

For this free-write, you are limited to fifteen to twenty words—like Gilbert's "Métier," previous page.

Is there an analogy you can access and use, as Gilbert does, to mirror the process of writing?

The form and subject matter is open. As Gary Snyder said at the 2009 Associated Writing Programs Conference, "Short poems are very difficult to write." So go easy on yourself!

7: Writing about Hardship

Imagine that food has become scarce due to a natural disaster. It is the second year of famine. You stand in bread lines, and sometimes skip meals to make your small store of supplies last longer. You drink water and crave juice. Protein is limited; fresh vegetables are limited to what you can grow in your garden if you have one, or buy on a good day.

Now write about this hunger for food as if it were

a hunger for words, imagination, and inspiration. Try to incorporate the sense of starving—the feeling of intense desire for a particular meal.

8: Writing about Exile

You are an ex-pat living in _____ (your choice of country.) Assume that you've been abroad for a year and will not be returning home due to ongoing violence and upheaval. Take a minute to ponder your situation and then write about your native land and your previous life there.

9: The Praise Poem

Write an homage to a particular poet, or to the poet as a universal figure, using Neruda's "The Poet's Obligation," below, as an example. Like Neruda, be sure to employ concrete images and avoid abstractions. As an alternative, write an "ode" or praise poem to (or in honor of) an object, a person, or a place. The form of the ode has been around for a long time, and means a lyric poem in the form of an address to a particular subject. This kind of poem is often elevated in style or manner, and is written in varied meter—it is, therefore, perfect for free verse or some blend of free verse with counted beats. In addition, it's a poem meant to be sung. Neruda's poem not only holds its music, it directly refers to various sounds:

The Poet's Obligation

To whoever is not listening to the sea
this Friday morning, to whoever is cooped up
in house or office, factory or woman
or street or mine or dry prison cell,
to him I come, and without speaking or looking
I arrive and open the door of his prison,
and a vibration starts up, vague and insistent,
a long rumble of thunder adds itself
to the weight of the planet and the foam,
the groaning rivers of the ocean rise,
the star vibrates quickly in its corona
and the sea beats, dies, and goes on beating.
So, drawn on by my destiny,
I ceaselessly must listen to and keep
the sea's lamenting in my consciousness,
I must feel the crash of the hard water
and gather it up in a perpetual cup
so that, wherever those in prison may be,
wherever they suffer the sentence of autumn,
I may be present with an errant wave,
I may move in and out of windows,
and hearing me, eyes may lift themselves,
asking "How can I reach the sea?"
And I will pass to them, saying nothing,
the starry echoes of the wave,
a breaking up of foam and quicksand,
a rustling of salt withdrawing from itself,
the gray cry of sea birds on the coast.
So, through me, freedom and the sea
will call in answer to the shrouded heart.

—Pablo Neruda, translated by Alastair Reed

10: Love

Write a love poem in which you address the reader in the second person (you). This voice can come in from the beginning, or it can enter the poem at any time, and leave as it pleases. As an alternative, use the third person (s/he, they) as the subject of the poem, and write about a person or place you love.

11: Find Your Process in a Season

For this exercise, try using the season or month of the year that holds particular significance for you. It may be the month of your birthday, or that of one of your parents or siblings. Or it could be the month you anticipate the most, due to the kind of weather that comes along.

Some people seem to enjoy 'weather' more than others—that is, wind and storm. They may be in the minority; certainly a fair number of folks look forward to summer time. But whatever season you choose, for the purposes of this exercise, entertain both good and bad aspects of your associations— the objects, scents, tastes, memories, and feelings about that particular time.

12: Exploit the Imperative

Write a poem about writing in which you address the reader in the imperative mood, that is, a poem that expresses a request or command. Feel free to demand both large and small things of the reader. An example of the imperative voice/mood follows:

"Read, every day, something no one else is reading. *Think*, every day, something no one else is thinking. *Do*, every day, something no one else would be silly enough to do. It is bad for the mind to be always part of unanimity." (Christopher Morley)

13: Risk Adjectives

Make a list of six things in a room of your house (or a childhood house, if you prefer to use your memory), that are ordinary and incidental. Then add adjectives to each of these objects—but find adjectives that are a bit out of the ordinary. Use a thesaurus if you need to, and try for adjectives that are concrete, specific, and sensory. Next, extend these two or three-word phrases into full lines, add a specific voice—yours, or another's. Voila, a rough draft may emerge.

14: The Letter Poem

Write a letter to your reader based upon and/ or located "in" a certain time of the day. You can assume your reader is a specific person and address this person, or you may choose to make your reader(s) a less defined, broader audience.

Whichever approach you choose, be sure to employ
concrete images that reveal the time of day or night
to ground the reader, as Billy Collins does in his
piece, "Night Letter to the Reader":

Night Letter to the Reader

I get up from the tangled bed and go outside,
a bird leaving its nest,
a snail taking a holiday from its shell,

but only to stand on the lawn,
an ordinary insomniac
amid the growth systems of garden and woods.

If I were younger, I might be thinking
about something I heard at a party,
about an unusual car,

or the press of Saturday night,
but as it is, I am simply conscious,
an animal in pajamas,

sensing only the pale humidity
of the night and the slight zephyrs
that stir the tops of the trees.

The dog has followed me out
and stands a little ahead,
her nose lifted as if she were inhaling

the tall white flowers,
visible tonight in the darkened garden,
and there was something else I wanted to tell you,

something about the warm orange light
in the windows of the house,
but now I am wondering if you are even listening

and why I bother to tell you these things
that will never make a difference,
flecks of ash, tiny chips of ice.

But this is all I want to do—
tell you that up in the woods
a few night birds were calling,

the grass was cold and wet on my bare feet,
and that at one point, the moon,
looking like the top of Shakespeare's

famous forehead,
appeared, quite unexpectedly,
illuminating a band of moving clouds.

—Billy Collins

15: The Light Poem

Write a light poem, deliberately. Or take a poem you have already written and "lighten it up"—like Miller's Light, Coor's Light, or "(your name) Lite." For this exercise, don't use easy humor—strive instead for the humor that resides in situations that seem gloomy from the outside but contain the germ or seed of comedy once one enters the action. Because humor is subjective, be aware that when you read this to others some folks may belly laugh while other listeners may not even crack a smile.

16: Get Your Land Legs

Imagine you have been at sea on a sailboat or other kind of boat—a yacht, even—for a week. The earth feels strangely solid and your body is still swaying inside. You enter your house. Write about the experience of returning from an aquatic voyage, using concrete objects and images from your home. Use your five senses, especially touch.

17: Controlled Rant

Brainstorm for a few minutes to come up with a random list of subjects you would not discuss with your friends and/or neighbors for fear of violating society's implicit conventions and mores, as described by Czeslaw Milosz' in his famous "Ars Poetica," lines 21 – 24, below. Once you have decide upon a topic, free-write in the first person or second person ("you"). Feel free to use any labels or identifying aspects of your chosen subject matter, but above all let your strong emotion drive the piece.

Ars Poetica?

I have always aspired to a more spacious form
that would be free from the claims of poetry or prose
and would let us understand each other without exposing
the author or reader to sublime agonies.

In the very essence of poetry there is something indecent:
a thing is brought forth which we didn't know we had in us,
so we blink our eyes, as if a tiger had sprung out
and stood in the light, lashing his tail.

That's why poetry is rightly said to be dictated by a daimonion,
though its an exaggeration to maintain that he must be an angel.
It's hard to guess where that pride of poets comes from,
when so often they're put to shame by the disclosure of their frailty.

What reasonable man would like to be a city of demons,
who behave as if they were at home, speak in many tongues,
and who, not satisfied with stealing his lips or hand,
work at changing his destiny for their convenience?

It's true that what is morbid is highly valued today,
and so you may think that I am only joking
or that I've devised just one more means
of praising Art with the help of irony.

There was a time when only wise books were read
helping us to bear our pain and misery.
This, after all, is not quite the same
as leafing through a thousand works fresh from psychiatric clinics.

And yet the world is different from what it seems to be
and we are other than how we see ourselves in our ravings.
People therefore preserve silent integrity
thus earning the respect of their relatives and neighbors.

The purpose of poetry is to remind us
how difficult it is to remain just one person,
for our house is open, there are no keys in the doors,
and invisible guests come in and out at will.

What I'm saying here is not, I agree, poetry,
as poems should be written rarely and reluctantly,
under unbearable duress and only with the hope
that good spirits, not evil ones, choose us for their instrument.

—Czeslaw Milosz

18: Creating Nostalgia

Think back to a moment in time and space when you felt acutely lonely, either as a child, an adolescent, or an adult. This exercise requires that you allow yourself the luxury of indolence, so don't rush it. Set out to remember the exact place where this experience occurred. As the memories come, perhaps slowly at first, and then with more intensity, use the first person singular ("I") or plural ("We") to merge the feelings you are having with those of the persona of "the poet within," as Hesse does in "The Poet," below.

For this exercise, as you free write, explore a particular landscape. Fill this scenery with palpable details indigenous to the place you have chosen. Use all five senses; be patient with yourself, and allow the place and/or time come to life. Then let the poem end where it wants to end. In other words, don't force a "Hollywood" or "pretty" ending.

The Poet

Only on me, the lonely one,
The unending stars of the night shine,
The stone fountain whispers its magic song,
To me alone, to me the lonely one
The colorful shadows of the wandering clouds
Move like dreams over the empty countryside.
Neither house nor farmland,
Neither forest nor hunting privilege is given to me,
What is mine belongs to no one,
The plunging brook behind the veil of the woods,
The frightening sea,
The bird whir of children at play,
The weeping and singing, lonely in the evening, of a man
 secretly in love.
The temples of the gods are mine also, and mine
The aristocratic groves of the past.
And no less, the luminous
Vault of heaven in the future is my home:
Often in the full flight of longing my soul storms upward,
To gaze on the future of blessed men,
Love, overcoming the law, love from people to people.
I find them all again, nobly transformed:
Farmer, king, tradesmen, bus sailors,
Shepherd and gardener, all of them
Gratefully celebrate the festival of the future world.
Only the poet is missing.

—Herman Hesse

19: Begin an Archaic Poem

For this free-write, get out a dictionary of ana-
chronistic terms, or call up online a list of archaic
words such as "amongst," "therein," "hereby, and
"whence." Picture a quill pen and an inkwell, and
write to your own imagination, addressing it from the
point of view of a pilgrim who has just arrived at your
own cozy writing spot. See the excerpt from William
Carlos Williams "The Uses of Poetry," below.

The Uses of Poetry

I've fond anticipation of a day
O'erfilled with pure diversion presently,
For I must read a lady poesy
The while we glide by many a leafy bay,
Hid deep in rushes, where at random play
The glossy black-winged May-flies, or whence flee
Hush-throated nestlings in alarm,
Whom we have idly frighted with our boat's long sway...

—William Carlos Williams

20: Pulling it All Together: Your Voice, Your Vision

Now that you have some fragments for poems—
and/or possibly a piece or two, here is a recipe
designed to assist you in creating your own ultimate
piece. Remember that it may take a few versions
to get there. Regarding the following suggestions,
as always, use the motto: "Take what you like and
leave the rest":

- Look back through pieces you've written and find a word—preferably a noun but it could be an adjective or verb—that you have repeated. Write this word down.

- Looking back at your poems, find the point of view you use most often: first person (I/we), second person (you, singular or collective), or third person (he/she/they/it). Make a note of this perspective, and use it as you write this piece.

- Choose a landscape as far from the one you currently reside in as possible. If you are a city dweller, this may be the country. If you have lived in many places within the US, it may be a foreign country. If you grew up in a rural setting but now live in 'suburbia' you may want to return to the rural setting. Write this landscape down, i.e., 'country,' 'city,' 'rural...'

- Think back to the first poem you ever wrote. What was the impetus behind that poem? Choose to be motivated by the same feeling—or a feeling as close to that as you can remember, if not put a name to.

- Free-write for ten to twenty minutes.

- Choose a set stanza length (from two line couplets to ten lines per stanza), and revise your piece.

- Let it age like a good wine, revise again, and send it out!

Poems About Writing Inspire More Poems

Poems written about the act of writing reveal the depth and breadth of a collective need to write. This material is available to poets who seek motivation. There may be no better way to spark one's own work than to read poems about writing poetry by other writers. This is what makes them "tick"; perhaps it is the basis upon which a sleeping passion can be remembered as well.

Perhaps it's presumptuous to say that if you read a poem or three about writing poetry during one of your "fallow" times you will begin to feel like writing a poem yourself. But it's worth a try. Delving into the process of writing can assist a foundering writer with the examination of his or her process. Add a bit of time and a place where you won't be disturbed—nowadays that is as difficult to carve out as the actual piece of writing—and you just may find yourself writing again.

According to Helen Vendler, "In the code language of criticism when a poem is said to be about poetry the word 'poetry' is often used to mean: how people construct an intelligibility out of the randomness they experience; how people choose what they love; how people integrate loss and gain; how they distort experience by wish and dream; how they perceive and consolidate flashes of harmony; how they (to end a list otherwise endless) achieve what Keats called a 'Soul or Intelligence destined to possess the sense of Identity.'"

This is only the tip of the iceberg.

Ars Poetica: The Birch

To hold as many lives, swirling
platinum-edged with ribbed bark curling,
sloughing like the empty, weathered
skin of paper wasp nests, peeling
within. And the arborist's scars stained
dark with creosote. The curving
cost of stubbornness, survival
highly overrated–perhaps–

This awkward, limbed ruin, ages
old, still sprouts trunk-sprung leaf buds
crowned with catkin-laden twigs, whirled
now with the unexpected *chits*
of small birds, wings sweeping too fast
to identify, welcomed by
more eyes than I can see. Hello,
dear visitants, uncaged–and quick–

—Christianne Balk

Why Write

Why else each day does the hawk fall
to its fierce grass
a clear and sullen line
talons stabbing once
aim true as desire?

—Michael Daley

Her

Is paints her
Is sings her and devours her
Is listens and sleeps
In the pliant rain of her feet

Is strikes and would descend her

Is plots is maps is invites is flowers
Breaks and borrows is lights is flies
Is fences shadows cries is dives and dreams

Her and hers are what poetry seeks

Sometimes I drive across town
For a few moments for a few words

It it is is hers and ever

—Kurt Olsson

On the Possible Utility of Poets

As we are affected and altered by the living earth,
I believe the earth is altered by the words we choose
to use as we experience its lives and its features.
          —Pattiann Rogers, "Under the
           Open Sky—Poems on the Land"
           Terrain magazine, Fall/Winter 2011

I propose new definitions of prayer:
Beachcombing. Birdwatching. Biking to work.
All times for the lost rite of attention.

How often is a star noticed in a night?
It matters. You need to know your family tree
of trees—which sheltered, which shaped you.

For lo, if I use crappy metaphors,
the first second or third easy thought,
the earth shudders, drought-cracks deepen.

Asparagus farmers are natural acolytes,
weeding around fronds luxuriant in dew.
Photographers too, especially those still

working with film, making pilgrimages
to the golden hour: *Film is a stone cold*
unforgiving killing bastard. Film is once

in a lifetime, no excuses, F8 and really be
there: steady, in focus, the shutter in synch

with life. The earth blooms a full inch
when my son notices, "A noun is basically
everything. We can't go anywhere without

nouns. They're always next to us," and when
my daughter asks, "What does the moon mean?"
and when I contemplate aqua, my favorite crayon,

its lagoons and flower centers, and yes even when
you give an extra paragraph of thought to your
deep love of chocolate-covered sea salt caramels.

The earth delights in how we enjoy how everyone
looks elegant skating, how that cinematic glide
puts wind in the hair, billows shirt sleeves.

To keep the earth fertile, we must endure rainouts,
put in time, keep observing, even humid days.
Smell the tiny tincture of home, the viny weeds

that grew in our town's grass but nowhere since.
Extra credit for mentioning hummingbirds,
for asking when it first sleeted, for imagining

a snow caterpillar, or lightning a foot deep,
Emulate the best disciples, who memorialize
small differences and rare views into words:

Marcescence: the retention of dead plant organs
that are normally shed, see oak, see beech.
Katabatic: of or relating to a wind produced

by the flow of cold dense air down a slope
as of a mountain or glacier. Paint a room
in the gradations of color in that sunset.

And maybe earth is an only child,
demanding attention, so long the one
planet supporting life. Small price for

the smell of hair just in from a winter
twilight walk. So I will craft an amulet,
silver exclamation point, her birthstone,

the amethyst, the dot, connected by audacity,
by the invisible pull of adamant reverence,
for all of us to wear and to hold, always.

—Tina Kelley

Ars Poetica

A poem should be palpable and mute
As a globed fruit
Dumb
As old medallions to the thumb
Silent as the sleeve-worn stone
Of casement ledges where the moss has grown—
A poem should be wordless
As the flight of birds
A poem should be motionless in time
As the moon climbs
Leaving, as the moon releases
Twig by twig the night-entangled trees,
Leaving, as the moon behind the winter leaves,
Memory by memory the mind -
A poem should be motionless in time
As the moon climbs
A poem should be equal to:
Not true
For all the history of grief
An empty doorway and a maple leaf
For love
The leaning grasses

and two lights above the sea -
A poem should not mean
But be

—Archibald MacLeish

Autopsycography

The poet is a pretender.
He pretends so thoroughly
That he even pretends to be pain—
The pain that he truly feels.
And those who read what he writes,
In the pain that is read they feel
Not those two pains that he had,
But only the one they don't have.
And so it is like this that on wheel-tracks
There runs around, keeping the mind busy,
That wind-up train
That is called "heart".

—Fernando Pessoa,
translated by Antonio Possolo

Ars Prosetica

I'd like to claim I came to poetry
Because the love of verse overwhelmed me.

Sure, in the sixth grade I memorized
"The Raven"--well, the first stanza. This disguised

In art my fascination with the dark
And strange. Every ocean held a shark

Back then. What else was all that water for
But to conceal a creature made of hunger?

The way they taught a poem in high school
Was as if it were some sort of puzzle:

The meaning trampled by the jackboot tread
Of the beat, hogtied in lines that knotted

My tongue whenever I had to "explicate."
Besides, who cared? I figured no one wrote

Poems any more. When Frost had died
In `63, that's what my teachers implied:

Verse had been commandeered by greeting cards,
And poetry hijacked by fuzzy bards

Like Rod McKuen who lapped their lonelymilk
In public. A real writer needed the bulk

And bite only prose allowed--this was clear.
Then a college prof read Kinnell's "The Bear"

Out loud: a hunt across a frozen sea;
A wounded beast; a man hungry

Enough to drink blood. When I felt wind
Sear my skin, my ears filled with the sound

Of howling, and I knew I had to trace
Its source. I stepped out onto that bauchy ice

To place my footprints in a world that grows
A rigid hide for the ocean coiling below.

—Michael Spence

Ars Poetica

My poems need to be more like a painting by Marc Chagall.
Where is the yellow cat mewing for milk?
Where are the lovers floating?

Faites Attention!
Watch out for the *Tour Eiffel*!

My poems need to fly out the window,
ride a beam of light until it runs into the spring
boulevards, the trees blooming and people
returning to *les Tuilleries*, *les Jardins*.

Ne march pas sur la palouse!

My poems beg for a beginning, *pain
au chocolat* or *brioche* with *du beurre* and raspberry jam,
a thick plate set on linen, red and white *fleur-de-lis*.

Secretly, my lines envy ribbons and feathers—
big plumes like the peacocks in Bois de Bologne—
and a French bulldog would be so *chic*.
Tout le monde has one these days.

My stanzas could use a new scarf, paisley perhaps,
and five ways to tie it, wrapping up loose ends
or settling over a lamp to make the mood.

Hungry, my poems crave a middle—
like Ile de la Cité, smack in the center of the Seine.

My poems would like to ride in *le bateau mouche*
or just lean back, look between
diamonds on the water flowing west
and the sky that might unfold in lilac
or green, an arc, a parade, a curtain of stars.

My poems want endings that sing
long into the night as the wind unwinds
through the plane trees, the wide-awake streets
a flute, a guitar, until dawn.

—Joannie Stangeland

Writing the Occasional Poem

A poem written to describe or comment on a particular
event, often written for a public reading, is known as an
"occasional poem." Thus, the occasional poem confers merit,
and in no small way can coax even the most reluctant, closet
poet, to re-think his or her recalcitrance, and get down to
the business of writing poetry. In this contemporary milieu,
part of the problem poets have is their lack of relationship
to the larger community. It could be that inclusion requires
an expansion of the poem's usage. How better to celebrate
poetry than to reveal, by celebrating and mourning essential
passages in life, its importance as a gift for those who most
require structure in a time of disorder.

There are many kinds of occasional poems, including poems about times of year such as the solstices and seasons, birthday poems, wedding poems (in the form of the Epithalamium) holiday pieces, and, of course, the elegy.

So without further ado, operating under the assumption that we, as poets, have an obligation to document, celebrate, mourn, praise, and otherwise break up the hum-drum of everyday life, select a person and/or an event you would like to write a poem for or about. It might be a birthday, a wedding, or a memorial service. Remember that poems can be written about anything, from the incidental to the serious.

Prior to writing:
- Take some time to reflect on the person/event.
- Make a list of sensory experiences unique to your own experience, those conjured by the season, if this piece will center around a time of year. It's helpful to do this even if the poem will not specifically address the calendar.
- Decide who your audience is.
- Choose whether you would like this to be a personal poem, or one that you will share with the audience you have chosen.

Three examples of occasional poems follow—a seasonal piece and an elegy from my book *Prisoner of the Swifts*, and a piece by Janée J. Baugher on the occasion of birth. As you read poetry journals and books, you'll notice many more examples. Almost every poet's canon contains occasional pieces.

October

And the wild rose
blooms again in stillness before rain.
October, song of my sister, of the psalms
said for gratitude against the coming

of sickness and gray days—one long day
lasts the whole of winter, one long night
that never lightens.
The wild rose strains to birth

one more blossom, to tinge the edge
of winter's sword with blood.
We who live in houses—
the lucky ones, we see and do not understand

men who sleep beneath bridges,
their heads cradled in cardboard boxes.
We know the tides come and go
as sickness comes and goes.

Our neighbor's bones will break and mend,
our children's children will fall
and be well. October, and the wild rose
raises itself up

at once plain and pretty
as if to right every wrong
done to the kingdom of ants and bees—
all those who live communally.

A Late Elegy

Almost December. A shock of blue
shoots from the hydrangea I planted
in memory of my father the astronomer—
his ashes, his stars.

Only one bloom this year.
Still it rises above black leaves
fallen from the apple tree,
whose naked limbs nod in assent.

The colorless branches trouble me.
I dream unripe dreams.
A stiff wind returns to the cul-de-sac
bringing its news—wax logs, sirens,

and cigarette smoke. I hear the whippoorwill
that should have left in autumn
but stayed on instead to winter in the yard.
I recognize this nocturnal, insect-eating nightjar.

I can't say which coast I'm on,
east or west, only that the water
has made inroads. Whippoorwill—its name echoes
its cry. The Jew who chose to be cremated

instead of buried, the man who could never
forgive himself despite all he overcame.
Poverty, stigma, the present of a broken pen
to his best friend when he was just a boy.

I fasten pearls around my neck,
my diamonds sparkle like his stars.

It's not so bad to be haunted by a nightjar
stuck to an apple tree. To be singular, or rich.

I watch the planets rise—Jupiter
with feathered bars, Saturn's mechanical rings.
The red shoulder and blue heel
of Orion tell me it is winter,

soon enough the doves will be driven,
like little sisters, from the sky above the gingko.
So what if my past
is prehistoric, if it nods and poses

above leaves cut in patterns,
yellow swans stuck to the earth.
What's left of my father—a hydrangea bloom
refusing to brown nose the cold.

The Newborn

Twenty-four hours old—
blond-and-cherry hair
indigo eyes you'll grow into.
Swaddled, sleeping babe,
finger-holding. Your long digits
with squared fingernails
already need to be clipped.

I press you to my chest,
steady the new neck
heed your coos, feel skin
as saintly as a foal's.
Your placenta's secure in a jar
and Mom's already ambulatory.

Six-pounder, teach me
grace of breath and being.
Your dreaming eyes
quiver under their lids.

—Janée J. Baugher

3. The Spark: Collaboration and Inspiration

"Shakespeare was initially more vain than proud;
at the end of his life—or at least his writing life—
he became more proud than vain."

—Fernando Pessoa, *Always Astonished*

Forgotten But Not Gone: Collaboration with a Photographer

The inspiration for *Forgotten But Not Gone* was the set of photographs Ron Hammond showed me. That work was done over a decade ago; the details of how we decided to collaborate on this project are sketchy. In any case, these short vignettes came easily.

I grew up in a "planned community"—Greenbelt, Maryland. My experiences there, from age six to twenty-eight—the at-once cloying and welcoming nature of small-town life—helped me to relate to Ron's photographs.

In fact, there was a "Co-op" in Greenbelt. Here is an excerpt from our book which makes use of poetic license to overlay a photograph of the Farmer's Co-op in Goodfield, Illinois, with the following aphoristic piece:

> "The Co-op once meant life to its members,
> even if that life was one where you could be
> accused of being a Communist, and taken in
> for questioning. Even when all that was inside
> the humble store answered *I'm not Red*:
> barrels of salt, sugar, and flour."

In addition, I'd spent two years in Westminster, Maryland at a born-again, jock/ROTC small university now known as McDaniel College. But for certain literature courses on Gandhi, and professors whose mentality rose far above the scenery of horse farms and poverty, I'd have been completely lost. That town had a railroad, silos, and abundant pasture land in the early seventies. In addition, I had visited relatives in the Midwest as a child, and found that I could identify with the landscapes. I'd experienced a squall and seen a tornado in the distance, and those images stayed with me. Ultimately, it became a gift to have visual point of reference to work with to access these "forgotten and all but lost" parts of my own past.

Latticework: Collaboration with a Textile Artist

I met Erika Carter in 2002 through the Contemporary QuiltArt Association. This organization had a unique and creative idea: forty textile artists volunteered to collaborate with a poet. Erika approached me after hearing me do a reading at the Bellevue Art Museum. According to a review in *Fiberarts* written subsequent to the finished work which was exhibited at the Hoffman Gallery in Portland, Oregon, and other national locations, "The quilt-artist poet pairs approached the project in varied ways...In some cases a quilt inspired a poem, or vice versa. In some cases the collaborators talked and emailed, exchanging ideas, each influencing the others work." (*Fiberarts*, 49)

Both of us found the inspiration was mutual. I set out to write a sequence based on Carter's "Time Series" and in very short order found myself with a book-length collection titled "Latticework." This manuscript was published in 2003 with one of Erika's textile pieces as cover art. Another five images appear within the collection. Ultimately, the work we did reinforces the words of participating poet Margaret Chula:

> "The words of the poem allow the quilt artist to look deeper into the fabric of her creation to see the layers that were not visible before. For the poet, words take on texture, color, linear rhythm—a rhythm of line and shapes rather than iambs. The sum of the piece becomes more than itself." (*Fiberarts*, 49)

What began as seeking common ground between us, and working separately in our respective fields to fulfill the collaboration project, became a rich, rewarding friendship with on-going collaboration in both art and life. It's this dialogue that nurtures the art in our lives.

Facing Page excerpted from
Fiberarts 2004, Issue 51, Summer

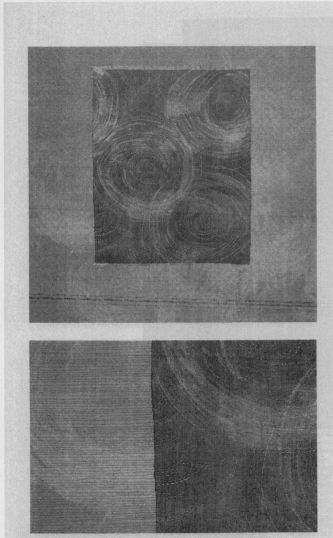

Erika Carter, Time Squared (with detail), 2002; cotton and linen fabric, pearl cotton; discharge, direct appliqué, machine and hand quilting; 40" x 41.5". From the outset, Carter and Skillman agreed not to "illustrate or caption each other's work," notes Carter. "We simply met to begin a conversation, a sharing of where we were to begin with. With time, we became aware of our similarities, which led to a developing relationship with subject. Our conversation continues today, stimulating new work." Photo by the artist.

MARKED

First by loneliness,
and later by the tastes
that come with the solitary life—
tea and chocolate, sugar
spooned from a canister
after granules turned into a drift
of snow, hard-packed.
You learn to scrape
leavings from the top layer,
you ration yourself, talk
to yourself about Jesus,
anything to keep the house
in place. As a singer marks
time with his voice—
one note, singular vibrato—
so you measure out a quarter,
a half teaspoon, and watch
something bitter grow
a little sweet. Only after
the kettle's screamed to itself
about boiling alone
on an element of red coils,
after the walk in the dark
down a street alternating
stars and neon. *The Church
of the Nazarene* sign buzzes
and, at the zenith, whatever
it is you haven't forgotten
or forgiven pulses. Perhaps
it's the Milky Way.
That flash—meteor
or torn retina?
Maybe the only way to tell
is to keep on walking,
talking to God
who lent his name
to every living thing
and then withdrew it,
come winter, leaving
on the objects—
lamp and spoon—haloed.
Holding the mandolin string
down with your third finger,
ringless. You know the book
by now—whomever you call on
will have also turned inward.
Each sliver of spare light
draws back from the sky
once the clocks fall back
in their places. You secure
the locks, call for certain
strays that earlier knew
what was leftover, what
the porchlight meant,
and how like a widow
a married woman
with grown children can feel.
—*Judith Skillman*

Tribal Moon Cycle: Collaboration with a Visual Artist

This collaboration was particularly rich and happened almost without effort on the part of the artist, Joan Stuart Ross, and myself. We'd worked together before on a public arts project, and had discussed trying another collaborative project. In the summer of 2009 I told Joan I was interested in writing about the Native American Moons, as they hold so many unique and evocative names for each month. She replied that she had recently been doing "moon" studies in her studio at Nahcotta, Washington. It was a wonderful coincidence!

As with Erika Carter, Joan and I each worked on our own and did not interact much for the first half of this project. I began to send Joan a few pieces, and she sent me a few, and then we got together. The set of poems and artworks in mixed media came together almost as if we were working on a mysterious and wonderful puzzle one afternoon

Ultimately there is incomparable richness to be found when a poet engages in exploration with artists in other media. It can truly be said the sum becomes more than its parts—joining with others can give you the spark you need not only to begin new work, but to see your material in a new light.

The best part is, all you have to do is look around. See what kind of art you like. Perhaps dabble in that medium yourself. See where it takes you—if you find you feel creative in another art form, don't feel this as a "time drain" or a problem. It's important not to hypnotize ourselves into the myth that verse-writing should always come first. Creativity is an abundant spring. To stifle it on any level interferes with the source.

Above all, don't be afraid to approach the artists and/or musicians with whom you feel an affinity. Many times you will find that they are looking for a way to break out of the isolation inherent in their chosen fields, just as you are.

Discussing Inspiration with Gloria Mindock, Editor, Cervéna Barva Press, (2006)

Gloria Mindock: Describe the room you write in.

Judith Skillman: I have written in many different rooms over the past twenty-five years. The common theme when I set up a "writing place" is a sturdy desk, a window, either with the desk facing the window or near it, index cards, my computer and printer, and my favorite authors in a cubby or on a shelf nearby.

Some of these are Philip Levine, Czeslaw Milosz, Frederico Garcia Lorca, Jorge Luis Borges, and Charles Baudelaire. There are many others, including the Swedish poet Edith Södergran. I often refer to Hugo's *The Triggering Town* and Stafford's *Writing the Australian Crawl* for inspiration, or during those 'fallow' times. The *University of Michigan Press* Series "Poets on Poetry" provides excellent essays from many poets, and has been a source of inspiration as well.

GM: Where do you find inspiration for writing?

JS: Inspiration comes in many forms. It can happen when I remember a vivid dream, have a conversation with a fellow writer or artist, or read an article, essay, short story, or novel. Dialogue with other authors and artists in diverse disciplines, including music and textile art, inspire me. Nature is another source of inspiration. I like to walk, either in the neighborhood, or on nearby trails in "Red Town," which is part of Cougar Mountain Regional Park. My walks aren't long. Just being around trees, plants, and, of course, the sun, is very calming.

Last but not least, my childhood is an endless source of inspiration. I must have suffered as a child, because I can never seem to get free of those memories. Writing about them is not only therapeutic, but creates a forum for me to investigate the past and see it in another light. I've not worried about "confessional" poetry—it seems to me all poetry contains potential components of a confession.

GM: You have two new books forthcoming by *Silverfish Review Press*, and from *David Robert Books*. Please give the names of your books and talk about your poetry in them.

JS: "Heat Lightning: New and Selected Poems 1986 - 2006" will be out shortly from *Silverfish Review Press*.

This is a collection of poems taken from my seven previously published books, plus a section of new poems that have been *in FIELD, Northwest Review, JAMA*, and other journals. I am very excited about this new collection as it feels as if a body of work has been completed. This project was demanding for Rodger Moody, the editor of SRP, yet he was very patient with the incredible number of changes that had to be integrated as we worked through the manuscript. Text is hard to pin down! "Coppelia, Certain Digressions," will be published by *David Robert Books* in the summer or early fall of 2006. This book contains poems about the myth of Coppelia, which was made into a ballet and is rather beautiful with a happy ending, and the reality of the Hoffman Coppelia story, which is not quite so pretty. The gist is that of a man who creates a woman and she becomes his puppet. I've tried to explore differences between the sexes in this book, and other themes as well, including figures from literature and myth such as Procrustes and Prometheus, and Madame de D., a young girl diagnosed with tourettes syndrome around the turn of the century. The poems are diverse, but I hope they hold together as another way of investigating both the dilemmas and delights of womanhood.

GM: I know one of the founding editors of *Fine Madness*, John Marshall. When did you become one of the editors? What sort of work does the magazine look for? Please talk about the magazine and the other editors involved.

JS: I became an editor for Fine Madness in the Spring of 2000. The magazine looks for accomplished verse with a certain flavor. Each issue has, on the inside cover, "Neat Marlow bathed in Thespian springs/ Had in him those brave translunary things…For that fine madness he did retaine,/ which rightly should possesse a poets braine."

We have published poets such as Neruda, Mandelstam, Keleras and others in translation. In addition, FM takes work from both well known and beginning poets from all over the country. Our editors are diverse, so much discussion takes place before accepting or rejecting a promising piece. I have found my work as an editor helpful in that it assists me in understanding the process that takes place when I send poems out in the mail. The work of a journal is intense and ongoing. None of the editors are paid. I suppose the reward is in finding a gem of a poem—those that make us go green with envy. And, of course, when a new issue comes out there is such a feeling of accomplishment. *Fine Madness* has received awards at Bumbershoot. It also gives four awards of $500 each for poets published in the magazine.

If Wishes Were Horses: Inspiration through Working with a Memoir Writer

FROM THE PREFACE

When I was growing up, my mother seemed to have a saying for everything that happened—good or bad. I had a difficult childhood, though I was told that "I was a happy baby" by my mother, but apparently that happiness, comfort and ease of life wore off as I became an adolescent in suburban Maryland, attending schools that did not do justice to a creative youngster, and far less to one whose coping skills were woefully maladapted to the diverse world we had entered. While my mother attended a school in which the girls and boys had separate classes, and one that was wholly Jewish and situated in her own neighborhood, I took a bus to a school whose student body was so diverse it made the word "melting pot" a euphemism for "burning syrup."

The net result of this bizarre difference in our backgrounds was that I became depressed, and when I went to my mother for advice or help she would always listen, give me a bear hug, and tell me she had confidence that I would work out my problems. Perhaps not the best assistance—my insomnia was severe by the time I was thirteen, but better than what some young adults receive from their parents. I did have an excellent role model in mom—she was confident, secure, and she had a technique for allowing sleep to come to her. It had to do with guided imagery. She would pretend she was lying on her back in the water—a lake or pool, and that relaxed her head to toe. In no time she'd be asleep, regardless of what was going on in her life. Our constitutions are very different, and I don't begrudge her rather succinct answers to my severe problems, except I do wish she'd passed on the stamina gene to me!

This collection of my mother's choice proverbs, sayings, witticisms, and aphorisms, and how they relate to her life, reveals a past much different than I imagined it to be as a child. A child or young adult growing up in a family sees that original family only in the context of her or his own limited experience.

Both my parents came from strong Jewish backgrounds, yet they raised me with science and analytic skills at the center of the universe, rather than the Old Testament God. I respect their decision, conscious or unconscious, to do this. The rift it created, however, made me wonder if sometimes I was going insane, growing up so differently than my peers, who had Christmas, and, for the most part, went to church or did not, but at least they had "holidays," and, from my knothole, that made for a more carefree and happy-go lucky existence than the one I experienced.

One thing I remember my mother saying in particular, and using a lot, when I came to her with my troubles, was "If wishes were horses, then beggars would ride." This cuts to the quick of many a child's deepest yearning for the imaginary, rosy world that adults know does not exist. Perhaps I wish she hadn't said it with such certainty. I would try to puzzle it out, and the puzzlement would become a profound confusion: what I want is not a horse, therefore, somewhere in the world, there is a poor person, a beggar, who can't ride off into the sunset. I really tried to fit my imagination around this proverb, to no avail.

After all, what is more important than wishing that

things might be different, and sharing in the idealism of youthful energy and disappointment this engenders? At the end of the day, however, now that I have three lovely, grown-up children and two grand children, I see in the seeds of her wisdom what she herself has sown.

From "Don't Look a Gift Horse in the Mouth"
When I first got enough distance to think back on my childhood, I realized that my parents were very poor when Ruth and I were born, and even five and half years later when Joel, the longed-for firstborn Jewish son, was born. There are two parts to this poverty that stand out for me. One is the fact that I never felt poor, even when we were living in a two bedroom, thin-walled townhouse, three kids in one room and two parents in the room next to it. Secondly, it was made clear to me from an early age that what is important in life is not appearances; rather it is what one does with one's life that counts.

This lesson was driven home again and again by both my mother and father. My father was a solar physicist at Goddard Space Flight Center, otherwise known as NASA, and my mother worked various jobs as a teacher, always full-time. I wasn't fully aware that part of that time she was in school getting her PhD, because I was too busy growing up and going to college myself, but

I suppose that her receiving her PhD in Mathematics Education exactly when I got my B.A. in English in 1976 made it very clear that she'd worked hard and long to achieve her personal goals in the field of education, and that education is extremely important.

Music was very much a part of the Kastner family while I was growing up. My sister, Ruthie, and I played violin under the tutelage of Dr. Berman, who was by all accounts an excellent violinist, but perhaps not the best teacher. He said "That stinks," and used other colorful expressions to urge us to practice more.

I did take a class from Dr. Berman at the University of Maryland when I fancied I might major in music one quarter, this idea having come to me sometime after Psychology, Fine Art, and later, Modern Dance; and before French film studies. I finally settled for a B.A. English, and went on to get an M.A. in English Literature with an emphasis in creative writing, as the terminal M.F.A degree didn't exist in 1983.

In any case, my renewed studies of the violin under Dr. Berman should perhaps have made clear to me that I am too shy to be a violinist. It took three more decades to figure that one out. I did, however, profit from the study of music in many ways. Of all the arts it is perhaps the least tangible. Much like writing, however, what is produced can be copied and distributed, and certainly music is the universal language for feelings.

I remember my mother receiving, for her birthday, a harpsichord kit. She and my father ordered it by mail—almost heretical in those days. It came, and they put it together. An exquisite instrument, it stood in the living room for two or three years. The endeavor of putting the kit together and having an actual harpsichord in the house generated the kind of excitement that still accompanies my favorite activities—writing poems and making stained glass windows.

When I think back to growing up in my original family, it is that honoring of discovery, art, and creativity—that nurturing of the spirit, that impresses me the most about my mother and father. While my brother and sister have the gift of analytic thinking that makes the hard sciences tangible and accessible, I do not. But there was never any disappointment expressed about this. Rather, I was encouraged to explore the strong interests I had. I was a voracious reader. As a teenager, I read Barth, Tolkien, Salinger, Faulkner, Hemingway, Roth, Michener, Kate Chopin—in short, anything and everything I could get my hands on. Most of my literature came from the Greenbelt Library. We didn't buy books, but I got some at second-hand shops.

This brings me to the gist of "Don't look a gift horse

in the mouth" and its meaning for me as an adult looking back on a lower middle-class childhood. Second-hand goods were commonplace in my house. Money was spent on observatory-building (my father was an amateur astronomer and took amazing photos of the sky with his own, hand-ground mirror and twelve inch telescope with clock drive—a whole other story) and violin lessons, and the occasional piece of teak furniture. Money was not used for clothing, frills, or anything that wasn't useful in the sense of being utilitarian as well as necessary for daily life.

I remember one summer my sister Ruthie, who had a passion for pottery, wanted a kiln. The next thing I knew, she had a whole ceramics studio on our glassed-in porch downstairs, complete with a potter's wheel, a kiln, various glazes, and a huge bag of clay. I was envious, and tried my hand at it, as, in fact I would do again many years later in my thirties when I took a pottery class at a local community college. I found I enjoyed the process, but it wasn't my niche. Her studio was proof, however, that there was simply no ceiling to which our parents would not go to support the creative urge. They would not, however, have a wet bar, invest in the stock market, or buy a new car.

This was in stark contrast to many of my friends, who had new clothes and lots of "stuff." If I wanted a skirt,

I would buy the fabric and the pattern, and make the skirt in an evening so I could wear it the next day. My mother, though she worked full-time, always had her sewing projects out on the dining room table on week ends, and she cooked up a storm. Things were home-made in the best sense of the word—made by one's own two hands.

It was a unique experience to grow up with such a variety of creative "preoccupations." I have no doubt that it has played a strong role in my choice of occupation. I am a poet, and that brings in almost no money. I teach part-time to have an income, but I'm lucky in that my husband has chosen to be the breadwinner for our family. His knack lies in that area. Mine does not. Due to the respect and dignity the arts held for my parents while I was growing up, I have never felt undermined in my quest for the muse. This thirty-year quest is not based on ambition, although it can't be completely divorced from a certain desire for recognition. Writing poems is something we do out of our passion to be the little god ordering the chaos that is life. The fact that poetry brings in little or no money usually doesn't trouble me unless I happen to get into a self-pity mode. Then I remember how valuable the lessons were, growing up in the Kastner household—"Don't look a gift horse in the mouth."

This gift, as I think about it years after first hearing the proverb, represents the act of creativity: the metaphoric horse. At the heart of the dilemma of living "the artistic life" are the horse's teeth, which are not necessarily sound. The horse, however, is real; it occupies space, wanders ceaselessly around the grounds prepared for it by solitude and reflection, trots in and out of one's life. If it happens to stand before me, hungry for to be taken in, I accept this maudlin stray with open arms. I don't dare look at its teeth: missing, broken, uneven. Even more, I am thankful that no one ever told me, when I was wont to spend whole days glued to a book, or to try a different instrument such as the flute, the guitar, or the viola da gamba, "No, you can't do that, it's frivolous." Rather, I was encouraged to experiment in any and all kinds of ways with the creative force that rejuvenates one's deepest self, even while lying dormant at times.

4. Your Poetry Manuscript

"It is the liberty to have a home of your own,
to do what you like in your spare time…"

—George Orwell, *Why I Write*

Revising Your Poetry Manuscript for Theme

When revising your chapbook or book-length manuscript of poems, begin to identify themes in your own work. While there are many ways to determine themes, let's start with some these definitions of the word "theme," from Webster's Dictionary:

1 a) a topic or subject...
1 b) a recurring, unifying subject or idea; motif...
3 b) a musical phrase upon which variations are developed...

The latter two definitions are the most important in a poetry manuscript. Then ask yourself these questions:

EXERCISE A:
- What recurring ideas do I see in these poems?
- How many poems contain imagery/metaphors for nature?
- How many poems contain imagery/metaphors for interpersonal relationships?
- Are there any cause-effect relationships in these poems or between the different poems themselves?
- Is there a character who appears more than once in the manuscript?
- If so, who is s/he?
- Is there a specific place where these poems are staged?

- Is there a specific time in which these poems occur?
- What recurring images can I find?
- What extended metaphors do I notice?
- What are my own favorite poems? Of these, which is my own personal favorite? (Note: If you have a chapbook, choose first a third of the manuscript, then choose your favorite poem from that selection. If a book-length mss., choose first a quarter of the poems in the mss., then choose the poem you feel is the strongest.)
- Which poem has the longest title? Which poem the shortest?

Once you have answered the above questions, you may want to begin looking for an "umbrella" poem, that is, a poem that is strong on its own and also provides specific clues to a reader as to what subject matter your manuscript will explore and develop. While no one poem can do this on its own, you're looking for the broadest hint at your material. A catchy title works to draw the reader in, while not giving too much away too early.

At some point you will want to decide where to place your title poem. It may be your favorite poem, the one that emerged when you answered one of the above questions. Remain open, however, as you work and re-work your manuscript, to the fact that your title may become another poem or phrase within one of the poems.

Identifying the Self

Another way of determining one's particular theme in a body of work is to study Roethke's memorable lines:

"I take it that we are faced with at least four principal themes: (1) The multiplicity, the chaos of modern life; (2) The way, the means of establishing a personal identity, a self in the face of chaos; (3) The nature of creation, that faculty for producing order out of disorder in the arts, particularly in poetry; and (4) The nature of God..." (Roethke 19.)

When a writer obtains the necessary distance to look back at what she has written, what often emerges is strong sense that the order a writer finds is more than a merely a device or afterthought of her work. Rather than being an afterthought, the theme contains the "aggregate souls" of the poet. In other words, the persona you adopt while writing can become the "raison d'être" for your uniquely original voice. Once this occurs, theme follows naturally.

This persona may be far stronger than you are aware of. It may be necessary to detach from your own work to evaluate the way in which you, the poet, have established a unique personal identity, as manifested in your work. That's where other poets, peer editing, and individual poetry submission come in. Editors can help you to identify those poems that work simply by making a comment on a poem, whether or not they "accept" it for publication.

It may be helpful to look at other poets' collections for the purpose of discerning their themes and exploring the reasoning behind the organization of poems and sections within a book:

> **EXERCISE B**
>
> Select a book of poetry by a poet you are unfamiliar with, and use questions from the Exercise A to analyze the poet's main theme(s). If you have a favorite poet, go online and order her/her book from amazon.com or barnes&noble.com. Browse a bookstore; go the library; find a book that appeals to you. Most libraries offer inter-loan policies. Expand your horizons as you hone your critical abilities.

Composing the manuscript

After you feel you have "nailed" your theme to the best of your ability given the existing poems, it's time to figure out how you can, using Webster's second two partial definitions above, allow this particular theme to recur within the manuscript. You don't want to have a part that is all about one thing. Rather, you want to subtly depart—as in a musical sonata or concerto—from the theme in order to return to it later.

In general, poems grouped in lumps or chunks of subject matter to begin with should, wherever possible, be given free rein to appear unexpectedly in the manuscript. The ability to see your own material impartially is important to accessing and achieving the "musical" variations on your theme. It takes practice. But it can be done.

Having a peer reviewer or an editor can be helpful when organizing your manuscript. It's important to continue sending out individual poems while working on a potential book. A comment from an editor, whether or not the editor accepts your poem for publication, confirms that the poem is strong enough to elicit a response. Finally, be aware that it may take anywhere from six months to six or more years for a "fledgling" manuscript to take shape and fly away.

An Interview with David Hoenigman

Note: An excerpted version of this interview from *Word Riot* is included here for its discussion of manuscript evolution.

David Hoenigman: What projects are you currently working on?

Judith Skillman: I am working on a manuscript titled "The White Cypress," which has as its theme the seven deadly sins. Not a pretty subject matter, but some of the poems had already been written when I recognized the theme/focus of my current writing. I decided to 'go deeper' into that realm, since I had already begun. This is often how manuscripts evolve, it seems to me—one is attracted to certain images and metaphors without knowing why. Becoming conscious of the underlying 'theme' takes time and can't be forced, which must be why writing a manuscript (of poems) takes place in geologic time.

DH: When and why did you begin writing?

JS: Actually, I wrote my first poem in fourth grade. It was an assignment: to write a poem about the assassination of President Kennedy (OK, yes, I've dated myself.) The poem was written in elementary school sing-song style, but it got recognized by a Maryland congressman, and was hung, alongside my fellow poet and fourth grade colleague Sandy Marion's. It was a very exciting experience for a fourth grader!

DH: When did you first consider yourself a writer?

JS: I began to think of myself as a 'poet' long before I had anything concrete to show for it. At Western Maryland College, now called "Westminster College," in a very sequestered town surrounded by horse towns and racial prejudice, I was first an art major. I had to make a change though, when we were forced to do architectural blueprints as a final project in a design class. I'd already taken a number of English classes, and was fascinated by "Beowulf," and Latin American Magical Realism. In fact I had been a total bookworm since learning to read at age six, so the change to English major was not difficult. What was hard was my art professor's dismay at my choice. He seemed personally offended. So I said "I'm going to be a poet," to which he replied, "Well then, that's OK."

DH: What inspired you to write your first book?

JS: My father was an astronomer and Solar Physicist, and my mother earned her PhD in Math Education, so my interest in Humanities made me rather a black sheep.

But they were encouraging of all art forms, especially music. Sometime during my youth my father ground his own mirror and installed his own observatory in our backyard. He loved to have 'star parties' and show off the stars to anyone who was interested. We also had discussions about the universe, or 'cosmology' as it is now called. So my first poems came from the excitement of discovery as witnessed in my father's excitement just looking at the night sky.

Then, when I became a literature major, and began reading poetry seriously, I couldn't keep from imitating those poets I admired. Imitation is discouraged among writers, but actually we can't help but do it all the time. Artists are encouraged, ordered even, to copy other artists as part of their learning process. So I think my unwitting 'copying' of styles allowed me, in time, to begin to learn what kind of voice I wanted to use.

DH: Who or what has influenced your writing?

JS: The excitement of waiting for a meteor shower, or seeing a celestial event such as a comet, gave me a bit of a drive to 'see' the unusual stuff going on around us every day. So my father, and my mother, who both always seemed to share in a child-like sense of wonder at nature and the world, were my first inspirations. After that, seeing and dabbling in visual art, hearing music, playing the violin—in which I was indoctrinated from third grade through high school—all contributed to my writing. One writer who has specifically influenced me is Beth Bentley. A wonderful poet and teacher, Beth Bentley has published *Little Fires* and *Phone Calls From the Dead*, among other books. She taught me to write "associatively." Though I had a master's degree and did a thesis (a manuscript of poems) for my MA at the University of Maryland, I feel it was Beth Bentley's verse-writing workshops at the UW Extension program, which I took sporadically, from 1983–1991, that really provided the most assistance.

Jack Gilbert is an amazing man, monk, and poet. He took the time to discuss writing with me, and I learned more from reading his work and talking to him about the difference between "fancy" and "imagination" than I feel I could have learned in years of course work. And there are so many other poets it would be impossible to list them. The pages of translations of César Vallejo, Paul Celan, and René Char are especially dog-eared.

DH: Do you have a specific writing style?

JS: I sometimes write in stanzas of set line lengths, or try for a three- or four-beat line. But my main goal is to have the content of a piece adhere to its form, and/or vice versa. The lyric is my first choice. I am always trying to strip language down to the essence in my quest for the minimalist poem. And I suppose that goes without saying, since poems should capture the essence of things. Certainly I live by several mottos: William Carlos Williams' "No ideas but in things" and Stafford's "Can't write? Lower your standards..." The latter has helped me through many a dry spell.

Ordering Your Manuscript: "Strategeries"

RANDOM APPROACH TO ORDER—THROW YOUR POEMS UP IN THE AIR AND SEE WHERE THEY LAND:
While this seems like a cop-out, what would be the advantage of giving this a try? It allows you to see that even when the poems fall into a random order, some sense of cause and effect still occurs. Why? Because everything you write has your own, unique stamp and voice on it. Therefore, you do not need to be too "uptight" about ordering your manuscript.

LOGICAL VS. INTUITIVE APPROACHES—TO ORDERING YOUR POETRY MANUSCRIPT:
Have you noticed a difference in organization when you put on your analytic hat vs. your intuitive hat? What kind of differences arise? If you lump all poems about

a certain subject matter, theme or extended metaphor (conceit) together, what happens? The result is often one of no diversion, no movement. Think of your book-to-be rather in terms of music as melody, refrain, departure, and return to the melody, Of course for this, as for every theoretical approach to art, there are exceptions.

NAMING PARTS—AND ORGANIZING MATERIAL INTO SECTIONS: How do you go about this?

First off, it's not as difficult as it sounds. Look for similarities between the pieces—is there water in a few of them? In more than a few? Does a character make an appearance in a few? Or are there similar landscapes that recur? If so, you've found gold! Go on looking for trends, as if you were a sleuth or a private investigator. Place poems that resonate in context, narrative, or elements (such as water, or a certain landscape, character, or kind of imagery) next to one another and see how many there are.

Does a certain phrase resonate for you from one of these poems? If so, type it and print it out and place it on top. Let it sit for a few days, weeks, even months. Then do the same for the rest of the section. A part break can contain as little as one long poem or five short poems. It can stretch to half a manuscript. The possibilities are endless. While organizing a manuscript, your job is to narrow the infinitely many configurations of material into a reader-friendly yet not overly "pat" format. Let the work stand out—give it room to live and breathe.

Select a strong poem for the beginning, and avoid the "prelude" or "preface" poem. Having a poem at the beginning of your manuscript, prior to the first section or the whole, if there are no sections, places too much emphasis on a manuscript and/or book-to-be. Sure, Billy Collins can get away with it, but normal mortals cannot. You want a poem that stands on its own but is "on theme." The ending poem, as I have come to understand it thanks to Jim Bodeen of Blue Begonia Press, should contain elements of awe. Jim once referred to a poem as a "prayer" and I think that analogy may be the highest praise a poem might earn.

In addition, the mid point of your manuscript is important. You don't want it to go "soft," or sag. In other words, you want to keep the reader's interest going. Consider making an entire section out of a long poem, placing the title poem there, or using an "anchor." If you think of the middle-point or mid-section of your manuscript as an anchor, then choose a piece that holds your underlying ideas—the "sub-text" that is crucial to your theme(s.)

Epigraphs

USE THE EPIGRAPH TO YOUR ADVANTAGE

Many writers use them, but not all do it well. How can you approach this? The most important thing is to understand what an epigraph is. All too often, this term is confused with "epigram," "eulogy," and other "e" words. An epigraph is a quotation set at the beginning of a literary work or one of its divisions to suggest its theme (Merriam-Webster); thus, there is no more perfect way to alert your reader— rather like a transition in a sentence or paragraph acts as a signpost—than to select a brief quotation that appeals to your sense of the work you will be presenting. Key to using this device is placing the phrase appropriately.

SELECT EPIGRAPHS TO CLUE YOUR READER

What might you choose as an epigraph if you had a manuscript about nature vs. man? What epigraphs might work well for other themes? As you read, keep track of quotations that move you. You might even consider beginning a log book or journal where you jot down possible epigraphs followed by the author's name and source. Some poets and writers use epigraphs on section breaks; some prefer to just use one or two on a page of the front matter for a collection.

Just as an academic writer doesn't want sources to take over his or her research paper, you don't want to lose your own original poetic voice to numerous epigraphs. But that may be the only way you can go wrong. So have at it! Use the work of others to open up aspects of your own writing. This is the beauty of literature—all canons entwined, all influences welcomed, all rivers running into the same ocean.

Creating Front and Back Matter for Your Book-Length Manuscript

SUGGESTED ORDER

1. You will need two cover pages. One should have your title in a larger font, bolded, but not huge: 14 point works well. It should also contain your name and address, email, and phone number. Avoid saying "by _____." Just put down your full name. Many authors prefer to center the title, and to place their contact information below, on the lower third/right hand side of the page.

2. The second page should contain the name of your title and nothing else. Note: There should be no page numbers on any of your front matter, though the page count does begin with the very first page.

3. Acknowledgements: This page should be titled (bold). Many authors make a brief statement such

as "Thanks to the following journals, where these poems first appeared:" Some authors prefer to add: "...where these poems first appeared, some in different versions:" or "...some with different titles:" Following the acknowledgement statement, you can either list your poems with the poem title in quotes and the journal in italics, and a comma between, or as a block. If you choose to group your published poems in a block form, use semi-colons between each poem and journal entry.

4. Acknowledgements for anthologies generally follow the same format, but appear after journal or other first publication sources, such as chapbooks.

5. Acknowledgements for those who have assisted you in writing and/or publishing your manuscript can also be listed, as well as any grants, residencies, and/ or awards that helped you to place your book.

6. Dedication: It is appropriate to dedicate your book to someone close to you, either living or dead. If you choose someone who has passed away, "In Memory of..." is a subtle but nice way to pay tribute. No need to use the word "Dedication" on the page, however.

7. Contents: To create your table of contents, use the "Insert" feature of Word Office Suite. (There

are certainly other options as technology evolves continually). As you scroll down, you will see a heading: "Indexes and Tables." Look under "Tables." The first time, your contents will end up in a random location, but then you can cut and paste it into the page following the Dedication. To make sure all titles of poems are picked up, use the "heading one" option under Word. To make sure section/part breaks are picked up, use "heading two." Questions? Ask your local techie!

8. Epigraph: Some poets like to include a brief epigraph just prior to the first poem or first section break. An epigraph is "a brief quotation placed at the beginning of a book, chapter, etc" (Webster's.) If you would like to do this, and have some author in mind, go for it. Any information that clues your reader as to your subject matter/tone/time period is invaluable in a poetry collection. (Note: no need to use the term "epigraph" on the page, but be sure to cite the material fully, using the author's name and the title of the work your epigraph is taken from. For more on the epigraph, see previous section).

9. Back Matter: It is appropriate to include a "Notes" page following your poems, especially if any allusions or vocabulary in your poems requires explanation beyond what the normal "lay person" would know. This is simply a reader- friendly way to include the

information without distracting your reader midway through your book, and/or including an awkward footnote. Scan through your poems and, if you see any words or phrases or poems that require a gloss, put the explanation on the Notes page. Generally authors try to order the notes as they follow the order of the poems within a manuscript. No numbers are required as long as a poem title or other identification device is included on the "Notes" page. It is even sometimes preferable, if you have dedicated a poem to someone, to include this information on that page as well. Then the poem may open up to more readers.

10. Biographical Note, or "About the Author:" Here is your chance to write a snazzy bio of yourself. Put in whatever feels relevant to you. Education is certainly important, as well as your background/home town. In addition, any awards you have received or previous books make a nice addition. Keep the tone professional, and try not to repeat your own name more than twice. Instead, use "S/he..."

11. Index of titles: This is helpful for longer volumes of poetry and/or New and Selected or Collected Poems. It can take a lot of work. Luckily, we don't usually have to worry about it. But don't rule it out if you are doing a collaborative work with another author or artist, a work of translation, or any volume over 150 pages.

5. Maintaining Motivation

"'…a man dabbles in verses and finds they are his life…'"

—Seamus Heaney, quoting Patrick Kavanagh

Join a Workshop

One of the best ways to progress as a poet is to surround yourself with other poets. Joining a poetry workshop accomplishes not only this, but provides many other benefits. From peer review to hearing your work discussed by other readers to camaraderie, there is nothing quite like the poetry workshop. A supportive yet honest critique of a single poem provides the writer with invaluable assistance for the revision process.

In fact, just knowing where a reader and/or listener gets confused enables a poet to go back to his or her piece and modify the language. There are many ways this can be done. From active development, in which you write more material and then pull missing puzzle parts across into your poem; to technical issues such as the insertion of a comma to clarify syntax, a workshop can be a source of renewed effort and enhanced creativity.

Some confusion is good, of course. Poems need not be overly transparent; their mystery lies in engaging figurative language and layers of meaning. According to Archibald MacLeish, "A poem should not mean/but be." Ultimately it's up to the writer to decide whether or not to entertain the comments given by workshop participants on a particular piece.

Sometimes workshops degenerate into places where members vote on aspects of one another's work. Like everything, a poetry workshop can have a life span. Some go on for decades; others, not very long. When devolution occurs in a workshop group, it can become painful to watch and participate. Time is valuable and hard to find for writers, who must often work full-time to support their vocation. Therefore, a workshop should not merely be a support group. A poet wants to have the honest reactions of his or her readers, no matter how strong the bonds have become between members. When a workshop becomes more of a polling event than a literary discussion, it may be time to find, or even to begin, another group.

Read, Read, Read

Writers begin as readers, yet often, as time goes by, we find ourselves neglecting reading. Apart from the sheer pleasure of reading, its importance for inspiration and continuing education cannot be overstated. David Wagoner, University of Washington Professor Emeritus and national/international poet, relates his story of being a student in Theodore Roethke's class: "Our assignment was to read everything written in the English language, during the fall term..."

Because the poet's medium is language, and language is fluid by nature, there are subtle and not so subtle changes that occur with time, especially on a colloquial level. Only by reading can one determine which changes are trends and fads, which are artifice (as in, devices and ploys) and which are ART—caps intentional. It is by reading both contemporary poetry and the classics that both the aspiring and experienced poet learns, is nurtured in his or her craft, and becomes inspired. Also, reading is one of the surefire ways a poet can develop his or her ear.

Finally, nothing is more nurturing to the spirit, and more helpful to continued progress as poets and writers, than picking up a book, or reading on Kindle or another online mode. Do poets always read poetry? Certainly not. Whether one's tastes run to plays, fiction, poetry, or non-fiction; to the literary, sci-fi, high adventure, or romance, through reading we encounter another's essence. Call it the *soul*, the inner vista of an author, what you will. Through the imagination, which is an aspect unique to reading, by virtue of endless combinations of characters in an alphabet, the reader is swept away. Inevitably the experience becomes one of not "When will I finish this story?" but rather "Oh dear, I never want to finish this book." Where else can we embark on a journey that defines and heightens our own sense of self even as we surrender ourselves to the page.

Marketing Strategies

If you wish to come out of the closet with your work as a poet, it's a good idea to begin submitting some poems. Here a few basic guidelines. There are many ways to market one's own work under the subject line "Shameless Self-Promotion." It's hard for poets to accept that the hard but necessary work of self promotion should carry no more shame than sending out a resume.

1. **Locate some basic resources:** Find these at your local library, or by browsing online:
    - Duotropes Digest: https://duotrope.com
    - Louis Crew's online submissions site: http:// andromeda.rutgers.edu/~lcrew/pbonline.html
    - *Poets & Writers Magazine*
    - *The Writer's Chronicle*, Association of Writers and Writing Programs (AWP).

2. **Take control:** Decide upon a set number of poems you will keep in the mail, and use that number. Often journals request that you send between four and six poems. So take the number twenty and divide by five if you wish to keep four 'batches' of poems in the mail; four if you wish to keep five 'batches' out at all times. Always keep a copy of what you send out via postal mail. Some editors will only send your work back if you provide adequate postage; more often now, the self addressed stamped envelope will

reappear in your mailbox with a rejection slip, or, preferably, an acceptance letter. Be sure your name and contact information appear in a brief cover letter or on a slip of paper, as well as on each poem you send out. Email submissions have largely replaced "snail mail" submissions—see #9, below.

3. **Use a calendar** to pencil in deadlines for grants, awards, and chapbook/manuscript contest you wish to enter. Use these deadlines as if they were in your workplace. Set yourself a goal, a contest to enter, and create the space to revise your manuscript or proposal and have it in the mail by the deadline. Keep in mind that most deadlines are POSTMARK based. List your goals for the coming year and tailor a plan to meet your personal goals, regardless of what the results may be.

4. **Tailor your marketing plan** to fit your own personal goals and lifestyle. Don't allow the marketing part of your work to interfere with your artistic space and sense of self. This means you must be prepared to face a large number of rejections. Even professional writers get many rejections. So persevere. Remember, you increase the odds of getting an acceptance by 100% merely by sending your work.

5. **Read contest and/or publisher's guidelines carefully**. Some first book contests, such as the Juniper Prize,

are held only every other year. Some grants such as the NEA for poets is available only every other year. So do your homework and use the calendar to avoid wasted time.

6. **Watch for burn out:** In the event you encounter a large number of rejections in a particular year or academic cycle (many journals, especially those associated with universities, are closed in the summer) take some time off from submitting and take a class and/or join a writer's workshop to focus more on process than end goal. This can take the sting out of the 'poebiz.' Or, as my mother used to say, "If you can't stand the heat, get out of the kitchen."

7. **Set realistic expectations:** Getting a poem accepted, even from a small journal, should be an occasion for celebration. You may have a long period of rejections punctuated only by a handwritten note on a rejection slip. Celebrate the personal touch; it is truly rare in the business of submission because editors receive so many 'batches' of poems and are generally volunteering their time and not getting paid. So while you may wish to be published in *The New Yorker*, an acceptance from a local journal should create enough affirmation to continue sending out. And certainly, if you get a personal note that asks for more poems, send more!

8. **Maintain control:** Use a log, either handwritten, or, even more user-friendly, computer-based, to record the name of each poem you send out and the journal name. You can also record the date of your submission and then, if and when it comes back. Note that there is a black hole in which things sometimes disappear mysteriously. If that happens, resubmit! You can cross off a journal that does not accept your work and send the poems elsewhere. In the 21st century, a large percentage of journals accept submissions via email.

9. **Go online**: It is likely your submission life will take you online, to sites such as *Submittable* and *Duotrope*, more often than not. Some sites allow you to keep a log of poems sent out, their status, etc.

10. **Submit to academia:** only during the academic year. This applies to journals associated with universities. Read about the journal to which you are submitting prior to sending. Many magazines will send sample copies for a minimal price. Be aware that some journals will not accept simultaneous submissions, that is, you may only send poems to them and you may not send the same poems elsewhere; while some do accept simultaneous submissions.

11. **Submit book-length or chapbook manuscripts**: Always send to more than one place. This increases the odds

your manuscript will be taken. Try sending "over the transom" to small presses, that is, don't go only the "contest route." Contests are expensive and, let's face it, judges are subjective. Each time you enter a contest, try finding a small press that is open to reading submissions.

12. **Is the glass half empty or half full?** Finally, remember to think of writing and submitting as you think about your life. If you get an acceptance, even if it is from a small or lesser known journal, celebrate, as suggested above in tip #7. Try to remain optimistic—remember that you are writing for yourself, and not others, and that even in choosing to exit the "writing closet" you still have a private life apart from anything less or more than a "big name" poet.

13. **Yes, really: it's half full!** Sylvia Plath and Anne Sexton and Hart Crane are good examples. Do you really want to be famous if it requires a bipolar, depressed, suicidal personality? Do you want to jet around the country and stay in hotels away from your loved ones for weeks at a time? Would your family and friends value you more if you were perpetually miserable about getting rejections? Undoubtedly not. So try to maintain perspective about your goals, desires and ambitions and to look at the big picture. In the business of poetry, the vast majority of poets are small fish in a large sea. The main thing is to swim.

How to Give a Successful Poetry Reading

Giving readings is another way to keep yourself motivated. Sharing poems out loud in a coffee shop, art gallery, or other venue allows you to measure your work in a way that can't be compared to any other. It's also a great way to meet other writers, sell books, buy books, and support the arts. Here are a few tips to help you get started, or remind you, if you're a pro, that it's OK to get a case of nerves.

1. Line up a venue. Check with your local bookstore, library, or arts commission.

2. Find out how much time you have to read and determine whether the venue needs a biographical note. If so, email or send a bio and/or photograph and/or other press release materials.

3. Plan your reading: rehearse the poems to be sure they fit into your time slot.

4. If you are terribly nervous about reading, do something physical before you get up on stage. Go for a run, work out, or take a brisk walk. Remember that adrenalin is the body's way of preparing to do a good job, so keep breathing.

5. If your hands shake when you read in front of people, type your poems out on paper and tape them to

cardboard. Cardboard doesn't shake and it is easy to manipulate in front of a crowd.

6. If appropriate, when you get up to read, thank the bookstore owners/reading coordinators/and/or person who introduced you. This doesn't apply to open mikes.

7. Take a few minutes to adjust the microphone, be sure you have your materials in the order you want them, and plant your feet squarely under your hips. Avoid long introductions to poems; rather, be succinct and give the audience any information they may need to better access your poem, including any notes or allusions.

8. If appropriate, introduce your reading by telling the audience the subject matter you plan to read, the book(s) or manuscripts you will be reading from, and/or any theme you have decided to address during your reading.

9. If you are nervous, begin by looking out over the heads of your audience. This creates a sense of availability in your voice and face while possibly masking a bad case of nerves.

10. When you feel comfortable enough to make eye contact, do so. But don't just sweep across the faces, find someone who seems to be listening and speak to him or her.

11. Intersperse "dark" poems with "lighter" poems for better flow.

12. If you get applause for a poem, wait a moment and thank the audience.

13. Remember to pause between poems even if there is an uncomfortable silence. This pause is like the rest in a piece of music. It helps the poem "settle in" for listeners.

14. Avoid disparaging your poems, either before or after delivery. Many poet do this, and while it is an understandable impulse, qualifying remarks diminish the impact of your work.

15. Read as if you are a musician. Allow your voice to rise or become louder during exciting and or faster parts of the "action"; let your voice fall or grow quieter while reading suspenseful portions of a poem.

16. Move around if you wish. Avoid beating out rhythm with your hand, although some poets do this quite effectively. You can move back and forth or left and right, and you can make some gestures without being a "performance poet." If you are in a situation without a stage and/or podium and you feel like it, take an opportunity to wander out into the audience. In theatre this is known as removing the "fourth wall." It seems scary but actually can be comforting to stand with those who have come to hear your read.

17. If you are angry while reading a poem you wrote while you were angry, you can show it. If you are sad you can also show it, though it is generally agreed that shedding tears is best reserved for private occasions. This rule has, however, been broken to good effect by at least one well-known poet in the Seattle area.

18. Let your audience know when you will be reading your last poem. You can preface the last poem like this "To close, I'd like to read a poem about..." You can also add, "Thank you for your attention" or "Thanks for listening," or thank the audience in any way you choose.

19. Finally, when you leave the podium or reading place, take all your papers/books, water, etc. Don't rush off—take your time. If there is another reader coming after you and you are the acting "MC," be sure you have information on how to introduce him or her.

20. Allow the applause to flood over you and pat yourself on the back. You've conquered stage fright. Each reading has its challenges. Avoid the temptation to flagellate yourself for what you did or didn't do as well as you wish; focus instead on setting up your next reading.

Allow Yourself to Lie Fallow

Everyone who writes, creates visual or sculptural or other art, or plays a musical instrument, eventually reaches a place beyond which progress seems not only impossible, but unimaginable. In musical training, this is referred to as a "plateau."

It's an occupational hazard of the writing life that now and again, in fact, sometimes quite often, a poet/writer feels unable to write up to the level that s/he has written before. That this is a frustrating situation is well known; much has been written of writers who had dry spells, poets who put their head in the oven and/or walked out into the sea in madness due to their manic depressive episodes which undoubtedly had/have an effect on that particular poet's canon/body of work (Plath, Roethke.)

What is less understood is the nature of the learning curve for writing in general and writing poems, specifically. In a workshop when I was in my late twenties at the Centrum Writers' Conference, Marvin Bell compared writing a poem to hitting a baseball, and suggested that, just as baseball players go out and hit the ball hundreds of time per day, so must poets write a lot in order to hone their skills. Even while putting in the best effort, however—using exercises, attending a class, either real or virtual/online, and applying the seat of our pants to the seat of the chair, poets can find themselves in that fallow place.

What causes this? It could be, just as in learning an instrument, that learning is still taking place. When I am "plateau'd," as happens more often now than when I was young and had, perhaps, more serotonin coursing through my body, I need to discover the right medicine for what ails me. Sometimes this means I need to stop trying to write, and concentrate on reading more. Often the battle takes place in another creative arena, perhaps playing an instrument, or singing in the shower. It helps to take up an entirely new creative activity, basically anything that involves the hand and the eye: sewing, baking, painting, cooking—the possibilities are endless. What matters is to become receptive once again to the imagination. Inevitably, once the pressure to "perform" dies down, that most plastic part of the mind will come out and play.

Court the Muse

The muse comes in many forms. When you feel you can't write, that's a good time to do something else that is stimulating and creative. Learn to play an instrument, try a new recipe, make a collage, take a watercolor or printmaking course—do anything that allows the intuitive side of your mind some latitude.

We are bombarded by information and tasks, second by second, in this 21st century. Creativity requires being in the present, and nothing beats music or art—visual, sculptural, domestic—to ground the body and free the mind. Some poets find it especially helpful to go on long walks. This has the added benefit of being good for one's health.

Suppose You Tried A Sonnet?

Why? To break out your routine. To change things up. As Ralph Waldo Emerson said, "…a foolish consistency is the hobgoblin of little minds." The issue of where to break a line is more straightforward with formal verse than free or open verse. The "end-stopped" line—which means the line ends with a distinct pause, generally with a period—becomes the norm. Rhymes, half-rhymes, or slant rhymes provide useful devices for breaking the line as well.

To learn more about forms and how to use them, see Babette Deutsch's invaluable resource: *Poetry Handbook: A Dictionary of Terms., 3rd Edition*. Many poets who write in free verse began by using forms. The exploration of form is essential to enlarging one's repertoire. In particular, since form and content should work together, a poem that won't work in free verse may be asking for a chance to become a sonnet, a villanelle, or a sestina.

Suppose you were to attempt to write a sonnet. If you begin working with this canonized, respected, both ancient and contemporary form, and then return to free verse, you might feel as if you have been set truly free. Give it a try. Use fourteen lines of iambic pentameter, with a rhyme scheme. For a Shakespearean sonnet, the letters below that are the same show rhymed, or half-rhymed lines:

A
B
A
B
C
D
C
D
E
F
E
F
G
G

In addition, there are many online sources that can coach you on how to write a sonnet, among them:

www.wikihow.com/Write-a-Sonnet
http://www.ehow.com/how_3335_write-sonnet.html

Here is an outstanding example:

Umbilical

—for my mother

Not flesh but string, the line which bound your foot
To mine, hobbling me so you could nap
And not worry I would wander loose
Those summer afternoons. But who could sleep
In such light? No boy of eight. I'd wait
Until your breath grew even. Holding mine,
I'd sit up slowly, carefully work the knot—
A ball of snake coils small but intricate
As trip-wires. One day I slipped the noose,
Eased off the creaking bed. Afraid you'd call
Me back, I tiptoed toward the doorway: no sign
I'd wakened you. I listened, then took a step
Through—and saw the darkness of the long hall.

—Michael Spence, *The New Criterion*

Is There a Poetic Sensibility?

Ultimately, in determining how much time you want to spend working on your own writing, this question arises. One would think for the question of such a sensibility to occur at all, there would have to exist an innate quality that makes a person want to write, or, the opposite, not want to write. But there may be an in-between ground as well—those who wanted to write and were discouraged in school or at other critical times in their lives.

Wallace Stevens put it this way in his essay "The Irrational Element in Poetry":

"A poet writes poetry because he is a poet; and he not a poet because he is a poet but because of his personal sensibility" (49.)

This quote, with its almost circular definition, is Stevensonian. In the same paragraph he also goes on to say that poets are born but not made. I feel it is important to offer a counterstatement: that poets can be made. The simple yearning to write is all that's necessary. Once the desire is there, the sensibility can be cultivated, just as one learns to play an instrument by practicing it.

Many writers become aware of the difference between feeling lonely and being alone. A fine balance is required to keep balance in one's life and yet carve out time for writing. The following questions are designed to assist you in developing your own creative sanctuary— the environment most conducive to freeing up your imagination and becoming prolific. While there are no right or wrong answers, it might be useful to record your answers. Again, these questions are merely to be pondered, as you take some time to create the place that *makes you want to be alone*. It is essential to have that sanctuary, with perhaps some inspiring books and pieces of art, photographs, and, if you are superstitious, fortune cookie inscription "You possess an excellent imagination"—a spot that tempts you to give yourself permission to simply "be," and whether you end up producing work that day or not, you will entertain the imagination with its infinite possibilities.

The Loneliness Questionnaire

1. Are there sensory aspects to your experience of being lonely?

2. How would you differentiate "being alone" and feeling "lonely"?

3. Do you feel lonely in a crowd? Always? Sometimes? Never?

4. Is loneliness a necessary component to the creative process, or is it counter-productive to the process of writing?

5. Would you ever go out of your way to feel lonely? Why or why not?

6. What is loneliness like for you?

7. Do loneliness and nostalgia go together?

8. Is there a time of day when you tend to feel more introverted? Likewise, is there a time of day when you feel more extroverted, social, gregarious?

9. If you are living with someone, do you structure your time so as to have time to yourself?

10. Under what circumstances might you prefer to be "left alone"?

Carve out Time for Writing

This stops some people because they set their standards too high. Why not try for just five, ten or fifteen minutes a day? And, as always, remember Stafford's words: "Can't write? Lower your standards." This is true for all the arts. Sometimes musicians, who must practice their art every day, must miss a few days. In that case, as a violin teacher once said "Just hold your ears and play the damn instrument." Don't feel that because you don't like what is happening, it means anything whatsoever. Feel proud that you are "applying the seat of your pants to the seat of the chair."

Equally important, determine your circadian rhythm. Are you an owl who loves to burn the midnight oil, or a lark, who rises before dawn and lies in bed with a journal? As a poet, this is one aspect of your body you need to understand. Fostering that time when you feel at your best with regard to being the little god who makes order out of chaos—that is, the writer—this is what will have the most influence on your creative process throughout your entire life. If you can exploit the rhythm to best suit your own body's natural functioning, well, that will be far better than fighting your way upstream.

The Gambit: How to Thrive on Submission & Rejection

The ability to do this is of paramount importance to writers, and to poets in particular. Because poets by and large are not paid for their work, as are essayists, non-fiction, children's writers, and fiction writers, there must be another sort of reward that keeps one going. Paradoxically, this reward must function in the absence of regular acceptances, pay, and pretty much everything society tells us is important. So how do we go about cultivating an attitude that allows us to put our work out there?

First off, the places to send out work has grown tremendously. There are thousands of markets in this age of email submissions, "Submishmash"; there are the long-time, established journals such as *Poetry, The Southern Review, The Iowa Review*, and hundreds of others. In addition, there are many new periodicals, both print and online. One can send out a submission abroad via email, thereby doing away with the old and difficult to use "IRC's" (International Reply Coupons.)

Within the range of expectations then, there exists the immediate gratification of an acceptance or the immediate downer of a fast rejection. To operate within this zone, the poet must develop a healthy disregard for the end results of his or her work. To cultivate this attitude, as well as to combat overemphasizing the reactions of the other to one's work, becomes critical to surviving in a world where millions of folks are producing poetry, much of it quite fine, and many journals are promoting works of poetry, without paying authors a single cent.

While there are no ready-made solutions to this dilemma, persistence is key. It's important take workshops and classes, whether in person or online, as interaction in the larger community of writers promotes the stability necessary to stay with the program and hone one's art. While receiving rejections on a regular basis can become daunting to one's ability to generate new material, a few supportive comments by peer editors can be equally encouraging fodder for the continuation of work on a new piece.

In addition, the more places one sends work to, the greater the odds of receiving an acceptance. In this second decade of the 21st century, most publishers seem to realize that multiple submissions are a necessity. Those who don't want a poem sent to them as well as another possible home must announce this in their journal or on their website. So keep a log, increase the odds, and accept that rejections will come. Because poetry is a subjective art, and editors are subjective, as are all people, receiving an acceptance can come down to something as simple increasing the odds.

And perhaps the only way to combat that down feeling that accompanies a rejection is to celebrate even the smallest piece of good news. It may not be an acceptance; it might be a more personal rejection, or a request to send other work. It could be a friend to whom you read your poem. Or perhaps someone whose canon you admire and keep coming back to for the sheer pleasure of reading.

It could be as simple as fighting your way through a difficult spell of writer's block. Keep coming back to the question "why am I doing this?" If the answer is "for others," you've chosen the wrong vocation, avocation, or hobby. Finally, remember that as a poet, while you may feel lonely at times, you are never alone. Reach out through your writing by asking whether your local newspaper might institute a poetry column. Find a community to sustain you through the difficult times and to help you to celebrate the unbeatable highs. Of course there is no stamp of approval, as each time a goal is reached, the ante seems to be raised. This inescapable fact is due to innate human ambition.

But remember, as a writer of the mysterious entity called "a poem," you participate in a highly original endeavor. Poetry allows for contact with the deepest self, even while it enriches yours and other's lives in the midst of the ordinary. There is no limit to the awareness acquired by a mind engaged in poesy. Of all the arts, it takes the fewest material items to perform—simply a pen and paper. The palette, instrument, clay, brush, carving tools—well, they are not required. All that is necessary to participate in this most ancient of the arts is an acuteness of perception, coupled with the desire to explore one's inner and outer landscapes.

Supporting Materials

Glossary

Alliteration: A repetition of consonant sounds at the beginning of words. Writers use alliteration for emphasis and to give their writing a musical quality.

Ars Poetica: A term meaning "The Art of Poetry" or "On the Nature of Poetry". Early examples of Ars Poetica by Aristotle and Horace have survived and have since spawned many other poems that bear the same name (perhaps the most recognized being Archibald MacLeish's modernist entry, ending with the well-known couplet "A poem should not mean/ But be"). While the term originated from poetry on poetry, it is now widely used as a literary device to enhance imagery, understanding, and profundity.

Beat: A pulse on the beat level, or the metric level at which pulses are heard as the basic unit. A beat is the basic time unit of a piece.

Blank Verse: unrhymed verse, especially the unrhymed iambic pentameter most frequently used in English dramatic, epic, and reflective verse.

Caesura: A pause in the middle of a line of poetry sometimes indicated by a punctuation mark, or simply shown by white space.

Conceit: A fanciful poetic image, especially an elaborate or exaggerated comparison.

Content: The meaning or significance of a *poem*, painting, or other work of art.

Couplet: A pair of lines of meter in poetry. It usually consists of two lines that rhyme.

Dash: A form of punctuation made by putting two hyphens together: --, or –.

Ekphrastic poem: A poem praising art—visual, sculptural, or art from other mediums.

Enjambment: A line that continues through into the next line of poetry, also called a "run-on" line. No punctuation appears at the end of this line.

Epithalamium: A poem written specifically for the bride on the way to her marriage.

Feet: In Western classical poetic traditions, the meter of a verse can be described as a sequence of *feet,* each foot being a specific sequence of syllable types — such as relatively unstressed/stressed (the norm for English poetry) or long/short (as in most classical Latin and Greek poetry).

Feminine ending: A line of verse that ends with an unstressed syllable.

Formal verse: Poetry that sticks to certain traditional patterns.

Free verse: Verse composed of variable, usually unrhymed lines having no fixed metrical pattern.

Free write: Putting pen or pencil to paper, or fingers to keyboard, and writing without stopping for a set length of time.

Full stop: The end of a sentence, or, in verse, the place where a pause or breath is distinctly felt or heard, as signified by a period.

Half Rhyme: Sometimes called half rhyme, near rhyme or imperfect rhyme, is consonance on the final letters of the words involved (e.g. *ill* with *shell*).

Iambic Pentameter: A common meter in English poetry based on a sequence of five iambic feet or iambs, each consisting of a relatively unstressed syllable (here represented with "×" above the syllable) followed by a relatively stressed one (here represented with "/" above the syllable) — "da-DUM" = "× /" :

  ×   / ×   / ×   /   ×   / ×   /
So long as men can breathe, or eyes can see,

  ×   / ×   / ×   / ×   / ×   /
So long lives this, and this gives life to thee.

This approach to analyzing and classifying meters originates from the ancient Greek tragedians and poets such as Homer, Pindar, Hesiod, and Sappho.

Line: A unit of language into which a poem is divided, which operates on principles which are distinct from and not necessarily coincident with grammatical structures, such as the sentence or clauses in sentences.

Masculine ending: Ending a line on a stressed syllable or word.

Metaphor: A figure of speech containing an implied comparison, in which a word or phrase ordinarily and primarily used of one thing is applied to another. Examples include "the curtain of night" and "all the world's a stage".

Meter: The basic rhythmic structure of a verse or lines in verse.

Open Verse: Also called "free verse" or "vers libre," this type of poetry does not use a rhyme scheme. It may use a number of beats per line, stanzas, or a concrete shape on the page, but there is no requirement for any set form.

Pantoum: A form of poetry similar to a villanelle in that there are repeating lines throughout the poem. It is composed of a series of quatrains; the second and fourth lines of each stanza are repeated as the first and third lines of the next. This pattern continues for any number of stanzas, except for the final stanza, which differs in the repeating pattern. The first and third lines of the last stanza are the second and fourth of the penultimate the first line of the poem is the last line of the final stanza, and the third line of the first stanza is the second of the final. Ideally, the meaning of lines shifts when they are repeated although the words remain exactly the same. This can be done by shifting punctuation.

Penultimate: The second to last line or stanza of a poem.

Prosody: The study of meters and forms of versification.

Quatrain: A type of stanza or a complete poem consisting of four lines. The most traditional and common are AAAA, AABB, and ABAB.

Refrain: The line or lines that are repeated in music or in verse; the "chorus" of a song. Poetic forms that feature refrains include the villanelle and the sestina.

Rhyme: The repetition of similar sounds in two or more words, most often at the end of lines in poems and songs.

Simile: Like a metaphor, a simile is a comparison. The primary difference is that a simile uses the word *like* or *as* to compare two things, while a metaphor suggests that the dissimilar things are the same.

Sestina: A structured 39-line poetic form consisting of six stanzas of six lines each, followed by a three-line stanza, known either as an envoi or tercet. The words that end each line of the first stanza are used as line endings in each of the following stanzas, rotated in a set pattern. The sestina is an example of a complex fixed verse form.

Stanza: A distinct numbered group of lines in verse; a grouping of two or more lines set off by a space. The stanza may or may not have a set pattern of meter and rhyme, depending upon whether it is being used for formal or free verse. The stanza in poetry is analogous with the paragraph that is seen in prose: related thoughts are grouped into units.

Stanzaic Verse: A poem using stanzas.

Style: At its simplest level, the manner in which an author chooses to write to his or her audience.

Symbol for line break: To indicate where a line should be broken, the back slash is used: /

Technique: Any standardized method an author uses to convey his or her message.

Tercet: Three lines of poetry forming a stanza or a complete poem. A poetic triplet is a tercet in which all three lines follow the same rhyme: *a a a*.

Villanelle: A nineteen-line poetic form consisting of five tercets followed by a quatrain. There are two refrains and two repeating rhymes, with the first and third line of the first tercet repeated alternately until the last stanza, which includes both repeated lines. The villanelle is an example of a fixed verse form.

Works Cited

Preface

Bloom, Harold. *The Anxiety of Influence: A Theory of Poetry.* Oxford University Press, US, 1997.

Hugo, Richard. *The Triggering Town: Lectures and Essays on Poetry and Writing.* W. W. Norton & Co., NY, 1979.

Preminger, Alex & T.V.F. Brogan. *The New Princeton Encyclopedia of Poetry and Poetics.* Princeton University Press/MJF Books, 1993.

Stafford, William. *Writing the Australian Crawl: Views on the Writer's Vocation.* Poets on Poetry Series, University of Michigan Press, 1978.

Letting Go and Getting On

Emanuel, Lynn. "She" from *Then, Suddenly.* University of Pittsburgh Press, 1999.

Epigraph from Roethke's essay "I Teach Out of Love," from *Straw for the Fire,* edited by David Wagoner. *Straw for the Fire: From the Notebooks of Theodore Roethke, 1943-1963. University of Washington Press,*1971.

"Epstein Barr," Judith Skillman, Poetry & Medicine Column, edited by Charlene Breedlove, *Journal of the American Medical Association (JAMA)* April 20th, 2010.

For more on enjambment, caesura, and end-stopped lines, see the website "Poem Shape": http://poemshape.

wordpress.com/2011/03/26/recognizing-using-caesuras-enjambment-and-end-stopped-lines/

For more on form, see Deutsch, Babette. *Poetry Handbook: A Dictionary of Terms, 3rd Edition.* Funk & Wagnall's, NY, 1969.

Gibbons, Reginald, *The Poet's Work: 29 Masters of 20th Century Poetry on the Origins and Practice of Their Art.* Houghton Mifflin Company, Boston. 1979.

Hugo, Richard. ibid.

In Alfred Kreymborg's poem, "Poetry," note that "Ladislaw" means "famous ruler" in Czechoslovakian.

Jim Bodeen is the founding editor of *Blue Begonia Press*, and the author of several volumes of poems, including *Impulse To Love, Whole Houses Shaking,* and *This House.* His work has been translated into Spanish. He edited the anthology *Weathered Pages* with Dan Peters, in which poems from The Poetry Pole were collected. For more on The Poetry Pole, see http://bluebegoniapress.com/poetry-pole

Mills, Ralph J., Jr. Editor: Roethke, Theodore. *On the Poet and His Craft: Selected Prose of Theodore Roethke.* University of Washington Press, Seattle and London, 1965.

Neufeldt, Victoria, Guralnik, David B., Editors. *Webster's New World College Dictionary*, Third Edition, p. 1386. Macmillan, NY, 1988.

Neufeldt, Victoria; Guralnik, David B., Editors, ibid.

"No ideas but in things" comes from the fifteenth line of the long poem *Paterson, Book I,* by William Carlos Williams: "—Say it, no ideas but in things—"

Phillips, Larry, Editor. "Ernest Hemingway on Writing." Simon & Schuster, New York, 1984.

Preminger, Alex & T.V.F. Brogan. *The New Princeton Encyclopedia of Poetry and Poetics.* ibid.

Roberta Fein's poem "The River at Albi" appeared in *Flycatcher,* Volume 2. Her full biography appears under Contributor Bio's.

Roethke, Theodore, ibid.

Stafford, William, ibid.

Stevens, Wallace. *The Palm at the End of the Mind: Selected Poems and a Play.* Edited by Holly Stevens. Vintage Books, Random House, 1972.

Strunk & White, *The Elements of Style*, Fourth Edition. Allyn & Bacon, 2000.

The actual quote from Anton Chekhov is more helpful than the slogan ("Show, don't tell"); it has become: "Don't tell me the moon is shining; show me the glint of light on broken glass."

The New Princeton Encyclopedia of Poetry and Poetics, ibid.

The word "Strategeries" is taken from one of President Bush (aka "W's") famous coinages.

Wallace Steven's essay, "The Irrational Element in Poetry," excerpted from *The Poet's Work*, Gibbons, Reginald, Editor. Houghton Mifflin Company Boston, 1979.

Your Poetry Manuscript

Epigraph from Orwell, George, *Why I Write*. Penguin Books, 1946.

Jim Bodeen, ibid.

"Ordering Your Manuscript for Theme," Mills, Ralph J., Jr. Editor: Roethke, Theodore. *On the Poet and His Craft: Selected Prose of Theodore Roethke*. University of Washington Press, Seattle and London, 1965.

Giving Writer's Block the Boot

Collins, Billy. "Night Letter to the Reader," *Nine Horses*. Random House Trade Paperbacks, NY, 2002

Gilbert, Jack. *Collected Poems*. Random House, 2012

Helen Hennessy Vendler, born April 30, 1933 in Boston, MA, is a leading American critic of poetry.

Hesse, Hermann, *Poems*. Translated by James Wright. Farrar, Straus and Giroux, New York, 1970.

Milosz, Czeslaw, *New and Collected Poems: 1931-2001*. Harper Collins, 2001.

Stevens, Wallace, *The Palm at the End of the Mind*, ibid.

Stevens, Wallace, ibid.

Stevens, Wallace, ibid.

Williams, William Carlos, *The Collected Poems*. New Directions Paperback, 1991.

The Spark: Collaboration and Inspiration

Epigraph from Pessoa, Fernando. *Always Astonished: Selected Prose*. Transl. Edwin Hong. City Lights Books, SF, 1988.

Fine Madness is no longer being published.

Kastner, Bernice Bloom. *If Wishes Were Horses: The Proverbs and Stories of Bernice Bloom Kastner.* Inkwater Press, 2009. Portions on Inspiration Through Working with a Memoir Writer were written for Dr. Kastner's book. They have been slightly revised.

Reproduction taken from Carter/Skillman collaboration: Patterson, Sunita. *Fiberarts* 2004, Issue 51, Summer.

Skillman, Judith. "October," "Late Elegy for My Father," *Prisoner of the Swifts.* Ahadada Books, 2009.

Maintaining Motivation

Epigraph taken from essay by Seamus Heaney titled "Feelings Into Words," *The Poet's Work*, ibid.

MacLeish, Archibald, ibid.

Milosz' biography excerpted from *Nobel Lectures, Literature 1968-1980*, Editor-in-Charge Tore Frängsmyr, Editor Sture Allén, World Scientific Publishing Co., Singapore, 1993.

Neruda's biography excerpted from The Nobel Foundation 1971: Pablo Neruda - Biography". Nobelprize.org. 8 Apr 2013. http://www.nobelprize.org/nobel_prizes/literature/laureates/1971/neruda-bio.html

Stevens, Wallace, "The Irrational Element in Poetry," *The Poet's Work*, ibid.

Author Bios: Poems for Jump Start Exercises

Billy Collins ("Night Letter to the Reader"), is an American poet, appointed as Poet Laureate of the United States from 2001 to 2003. He is a Distinguished Professor at Lehman College of the City University of New York and is the Senior Distinguished Fellow of the Winter Park Institute, Florida. Collins was recognized as a Literary Lion of the New York Public Library (1992) and selected as the New York State Poet for 2004-2006. He is currently a teacher in the MFA program at Stony Brook Southampton.

Brendan Galvin ("Ars Poetica: The Foxes") is the author of sixteen collections of poems. Habitat: New and Selected Poems 1965-2005 (LSU Press) was a finalist for the National Book Award. His awards include a Guggenheim Fellowship, two NEA fellowships, the Sotheby Prize of the Arvon Foundation (England), the Iowa Poetry Prize, and Poetry's Levinson Prize, among many others. Galvin has been Wyndham Robertson Visiting Writer in Residence in the MA program at Hollins University, Coal Royalty Distinguished Writer in Residence in the MFA program at the University of Alabama, Tuscaloosa, visiting writer at Connecticut College, and Whichard chair holder in the Humanities at East Carolina University. Currently he lives in Truro, Massachusetts.

Jack Gilbert ("Métier," "Doing Poetry"), February 18, 1925 – November 13, 2012. was an American poet who touched many people's lives with his lyrical voice and the luminous clarity of his work. Author of eight award-winning books, recipient of numerous awards including the Guggenheim and National Book Circle Critic Award as well as finalist for two Pulitzers, his audience continues to grow.

Hermann Hesse ("The Poet"), July 2, 1877 – August 9, 1962, was a German-Swiss poet, novelist, and painter. His best-known works include *Steppenwolf, Siddhartha*, and *The Glass Bead Game*, each of which explores an individual's search for authenticity, self-knowledge and spirituality. In 1946, he received the Nobel Prize in Literature.

Czeslaw Milosz ("Ars Poetica"), was born June 30, 1911 in Seteiniai, Lithuania, as a son of Aleksander Milosz, a civil engineer, and Weronika, née Kunat. He made his high-school and university studies in Wilno, then belonging to Poland. A co-founder of a literary group "Zagary", he made his literary début in 1930, published in the 1930s two volumes of poetry and worked for the Polish Radio. Most of the war time he spent in Warsaw working there for the underground presses. In 1960, invited by the University of California, he moved to Berkeley where he became, in 1961, Professor of Slavic Languages and Literatures. Czeslaw Milosz died on August 14, 2004.

Pablo Neruda ("The Poet's Obligation"), (1904 – 1973), was born in Chile, and became a Poet, diplomat, bohemian and political activist. Pablo Neruda was a household name throughout Latin America for much of the 20th century. In his 20s he was already famous for his Spanish-language poems of melancholy, love and eroticism, published in best-selling collections such as *Crepusculario* (1923) and a 1924 title translated as *Twenty Love Poems and a Song of Despair*. Neruda won the Nobel Prize for Literature in 1971 and died of cancer in 1973.

Wallace Stevens ("Poetry Is a Destructive Force"), (1879 – 1955) was an American Modernist poet. He was born in Reading, Pennsylvania, educated at Harvard and then New York Law School, and he spent most of his life working as an executive for an insurance company in Hartford, Connecticut. He won the Pulitzer Prize for Poetry for his *Collected Poems* in 1955.

William Carlos Williams ("The Uses of Poetry"), (1883 – 1963) was an American poet closely associated with modernism and imagism. He was also a pediatrician and general practitioner of medicine with a medical degree from the University of Pennsylvania School of Medicine. Williams "worked harder at being a writer than he did at being a physician" but excelled at both.

Contributor Biographies for Poems Included:

Christianne Balk's ("Ars Poetica: The Birch") books include *Bindweed* (Macmillan, Walt Whitman Award) and *Desiring Flight* (Purdue University Press). Her work has appeared in *The Alaska Quarterly Review, Alhambra Poetry Calendar, The Atlantic Monthly, Measure, Prairie Schooner*, and other journals and anthologies. Christianne loves broken music and riding her mother-in-law's thirty-year-old bike in triathlons.

Janée J. Baugher ("Newborn," *Tebot Bach*, 2013) is author of two collections of poetry, *The Body's Physics* (Tebot Bach) and *Coördinates of Yes* (Ahadada Books, 2010). She earned a Master of Fine Arts from Eastern Washington University. As an essayist, Baugher was awarded a 2012 fellowship at the Island Institute of Sitka (Alaska). She teaches literature at University of Phoenix in Seattle.

Sharon M. Carter ("Requiem for Agamemnon") recently retired after 38 years in healthcare and is keeping her promise to devote more time to the creative arts. Her visual art and poetry have been published online, in small presses and several anthologies. She received a Hedgebrook residency in 2001 and was a Jack Straw writer in 2003.

Michael Daley ("Why Write") is the author of seven chapbooks: *Angels, Amigos, Yes: Five Poems, Original Sin, The Corn Maiden, Horace: Eleven Odes*, and *Rosehip Plum Cherry;* a collection of essays: *Way Out There: Lyrical Essays;* and three collections of poetry: *The Straits, To Curve*, and *Moonlight in the Redemptive Forest*. He has received awards and grants from the National Endowment of Humanities, Fulbright, The Seattle Arts Commission, Bumbershoot, and Artist Trust.

Roberta Feins ("The River at Albi," *Flycatcher,* Volume 2) received her MFA in poetry in 2007 from New England College. Her poems have been published in *Five AM, Antioch Review, The Cortland Review* and *The Gettysburg Review*. Her first chapbook, *Something Like a River*, will be published by Moon Path Press in 2013. Roberta edits the University of Washington e-zine, *Switched On Gutenberg* (http://www.switched-ongutenberg.org).

Pamela Gross ("The Dark that in the Hemlock Hides") has been the recipient of numerous grants from the Seattle Arts Commission, the Artist Trust GAP funding, and King County Arts Commission. Her first complete poetry collection of poetry was published by the

University of Georgia, a winner in their Contemporary American Poets Series. *The Rules of Night Migration* was published by Paper Nautilus Press in 2013, as a winner of their 2012 competition.

Tina Kelley ("On the Possible Utility of Poets") published her second collection of poetry, *Precise*, with Word Press in January 2013. She is the co-author of *Almost Home: Helping Kids Move from Homelessness to Hope,* a nationally best-selling book about six homeless young people and addressing the forces that sent them to the street. Her first book of poems, *The Gospel of Galore,* (Word Press, 2003), won a Washington State Book Award. The epigraph for her piece is excerpted from Pattiann Rogers' "Under the Open Sky – Poems on the Land" *Terrain* magazine, Fall/Winter 2011.

Alfred Francis Kreymborg ("Poetry") was born in New York City on December 10, 1883, and died on August 14, 1966. In addition to writing his own work, he was instrumental in introducing the world to the Imagist movement through his journal *The Glebe*. A very prolific writer, Kreymborg was an American poet, novelist, playwright, literary editor and anthologist.

Sigrun Susan Lane ("So What Did You Come For") is a Seattle poet. She has published widely in national and regional publications, most notably *Albatross, Crab*

Creek Review, Malahat Review, Mom Egg, Rain City Review, Seattle Review, Sing Heavenly Muse, Spindrift, The Journal of the American Medical Association, Melusine, Pontoon, Ekphrasis, Still Crazy and others. She has received awards for her poetry from the Seattle and King County Arts Commissions.

Archibald MacLeish's "Ars Poetica" is a much-anthologized, famous piece. I first read it as an undergraduate and have enjoyed going back to it again and again. MacLeish (May 7, 1892 – April 20, 1982) was an American poet, writer, and the Librarian of Congress. He is associated with the Modernist school of poetry. He received three Pulitzer Prizes for his work.

Kurt Olsson's ("Her") first full-length book of poetry, *What Kills What Kills Us,* won the Gerald Cable Book Award (Silverfish Review Press, 2007). In 2008, the book was awarded the Towson University Prize for Literature, given annually to the best book published by a Maryland writer, as well as named Best Poetry Book of 2008 by Peace Corps Writers. Olsson's poems have appeared in many journals, including *Poetry, FIELD, The New Republic, Alaska Quarterly Review,* and *The Threepenny Review.*

Anne Pitkin's ("Man Staggering, Bronze") books are *Yellow* and *Winter Arguments.* Her work has appeared in

Alaska Quarterly Review, Prairie Schooner, Poetry, The New Orleans Review, Rattle, and other magazines and anthologies. Her current obsession, besides poetry, is playing jazz piano.

Antonio Possolo (translator of Fernando Pessoa's "Autopsycography) was born in Portugal, studied geology at the Classical University of Lisbon, and earned a PhD in statistics at Yale University. Translations of two of Fernando Pessoa's poems published in *Northwest Review* (1996, vol. 34, no. 2, pp. 61-65) are the result of joint work with Judith Skillman.

Michael Spence ("Ars Prosetica") has driven public-transit buses in the Seattle area for twenty-eight years. His poems have appeared recently in *The Hopkins Review, The Hudson Review, The Sewanee Review*, and *Tar River Poetry*. New work is forthcoming in *The New Criterion* and *Tampa Review*. A bus-driving poem of his was chosen as a finalist for the James Hearst Prize and will appear in *The North American Review*. His latest book is *Crush Depth* (Truman State University Press, 2009).

Joannie Stangeland ("Ars Poetica") published her most recent book, *Into the Rumored Spring,* with Ravenna Press. She is also the author of two chapbooks, including *A Steady Longing for Flight*, which won the Floating Bridge Press Chapbook Award. Her poems have appeared in *Superstition Review, The Midwest Quarterly, Valparaiso Poetry Review,* and other journals and anthologies. Joannie is an associate editor for *The Smoking Poet* and *Cascadia Review.*

Joan Swift ("Light Years") has published four full-length collections of poetry and two chapbooks. Her work has appeared *The Atlantic, The Yale Review, DoubleTake, Margie,* and dozens of other periodicals. She has won three National Endowment for the Arts Creative Arts Fellowships among other awards. She lives in Edmonds, Washington.

About the Author

Judith Skillman was born in Syracuse, New York, of Canadian parents, and holds dual citizenship. She is an amateur violinist, the mother of three grown children, and the "Grammy" of twin girls. She holds a Masters in English Literature from the University of Maryland, and has taught at University of Phoenix, Richard Hugo House, City University, and elsewhere.

Her latest collection is "The Phoenix: New & Selected Poems 2007 – 2013, from *Dream Horse Press.* The recipient of an award from the Academy of American Poets for her book *Storm* (Blue Begonia Press); she has also received a King County Arts Commission (KCAC) Publication Prize, Public Arts Grant, and Washington State Arts Commission

Writer's Fellowship. Two of her books were finalists for the Washington State Book Award (*Red Town* and *Prisoner of the Swifts*).

Skillman's poems and collaborative translations have appeared in *Poetry, FIELD, The Southern Review, The Iowa Review, The Midwest Quarterly, Ezra, Prairie Schooner, Seneca Review*, and other journals and anthologies. She has been a Writer in Residence at the Centrum Foundation in Port Townsend, Washington, and at the Hedgebrook Foundation. At the Center for French Translation in Seneffe, Belgium, she translated Belgian-French poet Anne-Marie Derèse.

A Jack Straw Writer in 2008 and 2013, Skillman's work has been nominated for Pushcart Prizes, the UK Kit Award, Best of the Web, and is included in *Best Indie Verse of New England.* For more information, visit *www.judithskillman.com*

Ms. Skillman is available for manuscript consultations through her website or *www.lummoxpress.com*

Other Titles by Judith Skillman:

The Phoenix: New & Selected Poems 2007 – 2013,
Dream Horse Press, 2013
The White Cypress, Cervéna Barva Press, 2011
The Never, Dream Horse Press, 2010
Prisoner of the Swifts, Ahadada Books, 2009
Anne Marie Derése in Translation & The Green Parrot,
Ahadada Books, 2008
The Body of Pain, Lily Press, 2007
Heat Lightning: New and Selected Poems 1986 – 2006,
Silverfish Review Press, 2006
Coppelia, Certain Digressions, David Robert Books,
2006
Opalescence, David Robert Books, 2005
Latticework, David Robert Books, 2004
Circe's Island, Silverfish Review Press, 2003
Red Town, Silverfish Review Press, 2001
Sweetbrier, Blue Begonia Working Signs Series, 2001
Storm, Blue Begonia Press, 1998
Beethoven and the Birds, Blue Begonia Press, 1996
Worship of the Visible Spectrum, Breitenbush Books,
1988

ABOUT THE LUMMOX PRESS

LUMMOX Press was created in 1994 by **RD Armstrong**. It began as a self-publishing/DIY imprint for poetry by RD, aka Raindog. Several chapbooks were published and in late 1995 LUMMOX began publishing *The LUMMOX Journal*, a monthly small/underground press lit-arts mag. Available primarily by subscription, the *LJ* continued its exploration of the "creative process" until its demise as a print mag in 2006. It was hailed as one of the best monthlies in the small press by John Berbrich and Todd Moore.

In 1998, LUMMOX began publishing the Little Red Book series, and continues to do so, sporadically, today. To date there are some 60 titles in the series and a collection of poems from the first decade of the series has been published under the title, **The Long Way Home** (2009). It's a great way to explore the series.

Together with Chris Yeseta (Layout and Art Direction since 1997), RD continues to publish books that are both striking in their looks as well as their content...*published because of the merit of the work, not the fame of the author.* That's why there are so many first full-length collections in the roster.

For a list of available titles, contact the LUMMOX Press via its website, *www.lummoxpress.com,* or write to LUMMOX, c/o PO Box 5301, San Pedro, CA 90733.

26564729R00112

Made in the USA
Lexington, KY
07 October 2013